Cambridge Elements

Elements in Epistemology
edited by
Stephen Hetherington
University of New South Wales, Sydney

THE EPISTEMOLOGY OF LOGIC

Ben Martin
University of Padua

Shaftesbury Road, Cambridge CB2 8EA, United Kingdom

One Liberty Plaza, 20th Floor, New York, NY 10006, USA

477 Williamstown Road, Port Melbourne, VIC 3207, Australia

314–321, 3rd Floor, Plot 3, Splendor Forum, Jasola District Centre, New Delhi – 110025, India

103 Penang Road, #05–06/07, Visioncrest Commercial, Singapore 238467

Cambridge University Press is part of Cambridge University Press & Assessment, a department of the University of Cambridge.

We share the University's mission to contribute to society through the pursuit of education, learning and research at the highest international levels of excellence.

www.cambridge.org
Information on this title: www.cambridge.org/9781009598408

DOI: 10.1017/9781009319881

© Ben Martin 2025

This publication is in copyright. Subject to statutory exception and to the provisions of relevant collective licensing agreements, with the exception of the Creative Commons version the link for which is provided below, no reproduction of any part may take place without the written permission of Cambridge University Press & Assessment.

An online version of this work is published at doi.org/10.1017/9781009319881 under a Creative Commons Open Access license CC-BY-NC 4.0 which permits re-use, distribution and reproduction in any medium for non-commercial purposes providing appropriate credit to the original work is given and any changes made are indicated. To view a copy of this license visit https://creativecommons.org/licenses/by-nc/4.0

When citing this work, please include a reference to the DOI 10.1017/9781009319881

First published 2025

A catalogue record for this publication is available from the British Library

ISBN 978-1-009-59840-8 Hardback
ISBN 978-1-009-31989-8 Paperback
ISSN 2398-0567 (online)
ISSN 2514-3832 (print)

Cambridge University Press & Assessment has no responsibility for the persistence or accuracy of URLs for external or third-party internet websites referred to in this publication and does not guarantee that any content on such websites is, or will remain, accurate or appropriate.

For EU product safety concerns, contact us at Calle de José Abascal, 56, 1°, 28003 Madrid, Spain, or email eugpsr@cambridge.org

The Epistemology of Logic

Elements in Epistemology

DOI: 10.1017/9781009319881
First published online: September 2025

Ben Martin
University of Padua
Author for correspondence: Ben Martin, ben.lj.martin@gmail.com

Abstract: Compared to our appreciation of the epistemology of the empirical sciences and mathematics, we have a relatively poor understanding of the epistemology of logic. This Element highlights three causes of this lack of progress: (i) failure to distinguish between the epistemology of logical *theorising* and that of good (logical) *reasoning*; (ii) hesitancy to base our accounts of the epistemology of logic on how logicians actually justify their logics, rather than our own presumptions about logic; and (iii) a presumption that the epistemology of logic must be significantly different to other research areas, such as the recognised sciences. The Element ends by highlighting what can be achieved by avoiding these pitfalls, presenting an account of theory-choice in logic, *logical predictivism*, motivated by actual logical practice, which suggests that the mechanisms of theory-choice in logic are not that different to those in the recognised sciences. This title is also available as Open Access on Cambridge Core.

Keywords: anti-exceptionalism about logic, practice-based approach, epistemological foundationalism, logical reasoning, epistemology of logic

© Ben Martin 2025

ISBNs: 9781009598408 (HB), 9781009319898 (PB), 9781009319881 (OC)
ISSNs: 2398-0567 (online), 2514-3832 (print)

Contents

Introduction	1
1 (The Epistemology of) Logic and Reasoning	3
2 The Practice-Based Approach	18
3 Foundationalism and the Exceptionality of Logic	31
4 An Epistemology of *Logica Artificialis*	46
5 Conclusion: *Logica Artificialis* and *Naturalis* Revisited	64
References	66

Introduction

Logic is often thought to play an important role in scientific inquiry (Maddy 2007). We rely upon it to prove theorems, test hypotheses, and construct logical systems to solve a host of technological problems. Yet, despite logic's prominence within scientific inquiry, we have a relatively poor understanding of its epistemology.

In contrast, within contemporary philosophy of science, one is struck by the wide range of detailed studies into the mechanisms by which theories are constructed and evaluated across the sciences. One finds investigations into the specific challenges facing climate models due to the complexity of their subject matter (Parker 2010), and how biologists simultaneously use multiple models to fulfil distinct predictive and explanatory goals (López-Rubio and Ratti 2021). Combined, these studies paint a picture of scientific research far more complex and multidimensional than traditional confirmationist or falsificationist accounts admit.

Yet, while logic is a human enterprise as rich and interesting as that of the sciences, none of the same positive conclusions can be drawn about our present understanding of its epistemology. Indeed, until recently, little attempt has been made to produce detailed accounts of logic's multifarious aims, the mechanisms by which logics are assessed, and the sources of evidence that inform our logical theories.[1] It is still common to find generic appeals to *rational intuitions* to plug gaps in our ignorance regarding logic's epistemology.

Yet, it isn't enough to recognise our present failings. We must also appreciate how we can do better. The objective of this Element is to do just that. First, by highlighting three prominent assumptions that have hindered the epistemology of logic's progress, and second, by pointing out (if all too briefly) what can be achieved once we avoid these pitfalls.

We begin, in Section 1, with the mistake sometimes made of confusing the epistemology of *logic* for the epistemology of *(good) reasoning*. It is often claimed that logic is the study of good reasoning, and it's true that this understanding of logic has held an important role in its development. However, even *if* logic is the study of good reasoning, this does not entail that the *epistemology* of logic is equivalent to the *epistemology* of good reasoning. Conceiving of the epistemology of logic as just the epistemology of good reasoning has led to an often-singular focus on specifying the conditions under which someone is

---

[1] A keen-eyed reader may notice we have used the term 'logic' to refer variously to the *research field of* logic, the *mathematical objects* used by the field, and the *subject matter* logic of the field. This is no sleight of hand. As we'll see, while it's important to distinguish between these three senses of 'logic', each has a role to play in understanding the epistemology of *logic*.

justified in making a certain type of inference. Yet, it's one matter for logic to have *implications* for good (deductive) reasoning, and another to think that the epistemology of how we discover and justify these logical laws is equivalent to the conditions under which someone is justified in making an inference. This would be akin to reducing the epistemology of the axioms of arithmetic to that of accurate counting or summation. We end the section by outlining the benefits of focusing on the epistemology of logic as a separate enterprise from that of (good) reasoning.

Section 2 moves on to our second mistake, which is to presume that the most suitable philosophical method to construct an epistemology of logic is to deduce it from our own assumptions about the nature of logic, knowledge, and rationality more generally. This is known as a *top-down* approach to the epistemology of a field; one begins with certain (reasonable) assumptions about the field and other claims we take ourselves to know, and from these infers what the epistemology of the field *should* look like given these facts. It is such an approach that has produced many of the traditional epistemologies of science and mathematics, such as Popper's falsificationism. Unfortunately, what tends to result from this approach are oversimplified pictures of the field's epistemology. The same is true when it comes to logic.

To address this mistake, we need a shift away from top-down approaches towards a *bottom-up* approach, in which epistemologies of logic are built up from case studies of how logicians go about developing and justifying their theories. In other words, we treat the practice of logicians as a reliable guide to what constitutes logic's epistemology, just as we treat the activities of scientists as the most reliable guide we have to how the scientific method operates. This methodology, known as the *practice-based approach*, is at the root of much of the progress recently made within the philosophy of science.

Section 3 discusses the third and final mistake to avoid, which is to presume that the epistemology of logic must be *wholly different* from that of other research areas, particularly the recognised sciences. Of course, given that each research area has its own peculiar subject matter and research goals, we would expect the methodological norms of each field to reflect these goals and the features of its subject matter. However, when it comes to logic, the traditional expectation is that logic's epistemology is wholly different from that of other areas, based upon its *foundational status* in inquiry. What results is a form of epistemic foundationalism, in which at least a subset of the logical laws must be non-inferentially accessible to us, whether through rational insight or analyticity. Here we show that, once we consider how logicians actually go about justifying their logics, it's clear we do not have direct access to the logical laws (even fallibly). While it's perfectly acceptable to propose differences between the epistemology of logic and the recognised sciences, such proposals should not be axioms based upon philosophical presumptions but rather justified by the realities of research in the field.

To show the benefits of avoiding these pitfalls, the final section presents an epistemology of logic, *logical predictivism*, which makes none of these mistakes. According to predictivism, logics are justified by their predictive success, explanatory power, and compatibility with other well-evidenced commitments. It does not presume that an epistemology of logic is equivalent to an epistemology of reasoning (even *if* logic is in some sense the study of good reasoning), or that its epistemology must be wholly different from that of other research areas (though it will still have its own particular features), and it is justified not on the basis of presumptions about what we think logic's epistemology *should* look like, but rather on how logics actually are justified in the field.

Understanding the epistemology of logic is important not only because of some professional embarrassment philosophers of logic may feel when they see the comparative successes philosophers of science have achieved. Possessing an understanding of what makes logics successful has clear practical motivations. For all of classical logic's success, the last sixty years have seen a proliferation of non-classical logics, including paraconsistent, substructural, and constructivist. Each with its own motivations, whether addressing a logico-semantic paradox, concerns over vagueness, or the nature of mathematical inquiry.

Of course, despite the rise in non-classical competitors, classical logic may indeed be correct; after all, it has been a remarkably successful theory. However, its continued success (and truth) is not assured. While our period is hardly one of scientific crisis, it is one of logical *plenitude*. With the abundance of logics available to us, we have the need to assess which is best suited to our theoretical goals. Given this, just as during periods of revolution in the sciences, when attention was focused on fundamental epistemological questions about the field, so it is appropriate to do so now with logic. Only then can we understand why some logics are better than others.

To even engage in understanding these processes and why we value certain logics, however, it is paramount that we give the epistemology of *logic* its own attention, apart from that of (good) reasoning. For this reason, we begin with a discussion of this distinction.

1 (The Epistemology of) Logic and Reasoning

Talk of 'logic' is ambiguous, and so talk of the *epistemology of* logic is bound to derivatively contain ambiguities. Within different contexts, we happily use the term 'logic' to refer to: (i) the *research area* itself, practiced across philosophy, mathematics, and computer science departments; (ii) the *objects*, in this case mathematical systems and tools, which logicians produce; and (iii) the *subject matter(s)* of the research area.

Yet, inevitably, one's use of the term will impact one's answer to what constitutes the epistemology of *logic*. In particular, confining one's understanding of 'logic' to a specific subject matter within the research area will restrict one's focus to the epistemology of this putative subject matter. This sometimes occurs in contemporary debates over logic's epistemology, where attention has primarily been given to the epistemology of *good reasoning*. While this focus is understandable, as it's a long-standing presumption that the primary purpose of logic is determining the rules for *good* reasoning, it ultimately limits our understanding of logic's epistemology.

Our goal in this section is twofold. First, to warn against equating the epistemology of logic with the epistemology of what is often taken to be its primary subject matter – good reasoning. Even if logic, properly understood, is the study of the laws of good reasoning, this does not mean the *epistemology* of logic equates to the *epistemology* of good reasoning. To show this, we distinguish five levels of 'logical' justification, each requiring a greater degree of understanding than the prior, ranging from being able to *reliably make* logical inferences at one end of the spectrum to being justified in endorsing a logic at the other. Further, we show that the conditions for possessing justification at each level do not suffice for the next. Thus, understanding the epistemology of each level is a discrete endeavour. This highlights the importance of separating two distinct projects: (i) providing an epistemology for *good* (putatively logical) *reasoning*, and (ii) an epistemology for *logical theorising*.

Second, we point out that, in order to answer important questions about the nature of logic, there are compelling reasons not to restrict ourselves to the epistemology of *good* reasoning but rather to attend to more theoretical forms of logical justification. This forms the basis of our decision in this Element to focus on the epistemology of logic understood in this more theoretical sense: what we will call *logica artificialis*. To understand how this equivocation came about, it will help to begin with a brief historical detour.

1.1 Logic as a Science and Instrument for Good Reasoning

The proposal that logic is the study of *good reasoning* has its basis in the birth of the systematic study of logical rules in Ancient Greece. During this period, logic covered a wider range of topics than formal logic does now, including dialectic, rhetoric, and the assessment of definitions. However, as is the case now, logic was given the dual task of acting both as an *instrument* for good reasoning and as an independent area of philosophy studying these principles:

> [Logic originated as] a science to discriminate between what is true and what is false, and to show which reasoning really adheres to the path of valid argumentative proof... Among the various branches of philosophy, logic has two prerogatives: it has both the honour of coming first and the distinction of serving as an efficacious instrument throughout the whole body. (John of Salisbury 1955: II.2–5)

To clarify these roles, philosophers in the later Middle Ages introduced a distinction between (i) *logica naturalis*, the norms of reasoning humans actually follow, and (ii) *logica artificialis*, the rules laid down by the field of logic (Hoenen 2010). While *logica artificialis* constituted a science (*scientia*) in its own right, with its own distinct subject matter, the laws it produced were expected to inform our actual reasoning processes (*logica naturalis*).[2] In other words, logic was both a *science* and an *instrument*. The question, then, was the extent to which the *logica artificialis* of the day, the syllogistic, served this instrumental role successfully.

Both Descartes and Bacon famously criticised syllogistic logic for failing to be an effective organon. While for Descartes, the forms were at best pedagogical tools for those still honing their intellectual abilities, not useful for the already logically clear-minded, for Bacon, the forms were useless in providing natural philosophers with the means to make novel discoveries; hence the need for a *new Organon* (Gaukroger 1989).

Similarly, Locke (1975 [1689]: IV.xvii) criticised the forms for adding little to our understanding of whether a particular argument is (in)valid. Rather, they are mere codifications of those arguments we *already* deem reasonable through appreciating the relations between the ideas contained within them. So, if one does not find the instances of the syllogistic forms reasonable to begin with, the forms themselves will have little elucidatory force. Thus, while correct as *codifications* of these existent acceptable inferences (logic's role *qua* science), the forms fail to serve logic's instrumental role.

Logic's dual life is also apparent in the work of advocates for *logica artificialis*, who defended the science on the basis that it *could* effectively guide reasoning. That artificial logics are needed to regulate our existing inferential standards and avoid unnecessary errors:

---

[2] Calling logic a *scientiam* in the medieval sense of the term should not be confused with the contemporary thesis that logic is akin to the sciences in various regards, known as *anti-exceptionalism about logic* (Martin & Hjortland 2022). Rather, *scientiae* were simply systematic bodies of truths with their own subject matter, derivable from a set of foundational principles.

> For when natural good sense undertakes to analyse a piece of reasoning without help from the art [of logic], it will sometimes be in a little difficulty about the validity of the inferences – finding for example that the reasoning involves some [syllogistic] mood which is indeed sound but which is not in common use. (Leibniz 1996 [1765]: IV 481)

Thus, even for the most avid advocate of formal logic during this period, *logica artificialis* was recognised as important not only because it constituted the study of correct arguments, but because it served as an effective instrument for *logica naturalis*.

This historical context is instructive in two respects. First, it helps us appreciate why contemporary philosophy places such importance on logic's instrumental value in informing reasoning, even using this instrumental purpose to define logic's *subject matter*. For instance, contemporary authors often propose the study of (a subclass of) good reasoning as the *canonical* application of logic (Cook 2010; Priest 2006a).[3]

While the terms *logica artificialis* and *naturalis* have now exited our lexicon, replaced by *formal logic* and *reasoning*, respectively, there is still the expectation that the fruits of the former inform the latter.[4] Thus, even if logics understood as mathematical calculi are now put to many purposes – including modelling meaning composition (Dalrymple 2001) and national incomes (Ferrer-Comalat et al. 2020) – it is common to hear that the *philosophically primary* application of our logics (the products of *logica artificialis*) is to reasoning, allowing us to identify reasoning which is *logically good*, or, for short, 'logical'.

Second, acknowledging this dual role of *logica artificialis* as its own science and as an instrument for reasoning goes some way towards explaining how equivocations of 'epistemology of *logic*' have occurred, with the adjective 'logical' being equally applied to those pieces of natural-language reasoning that formal logics purportedly sanction. For instance, the inference to 'I'll go to

---

[3] Why the study of a *subclass of* good reasoning and not *all* such reasoning? From at least the fourteenth century onwards, it has generally been accepted that *logical* rules do not account for all instances of good reasoning, even focusing on *deductively* good reasoning (Mugnai 2010). There are certain inferences that while *mathematically* or *lexically* acceptable from a deductive point of view are not *logically valid*. The matter of what constitutes this distinction between logical and non-logical forms of reasoning is less obvious. While it often has to do with considerations of *formality, generality* and *topic-neutrality*, discussing the exact rationale here would take us too far afield (cf. Sher 1991).

[4] To *what extent* exactly is a live debate, restarted by Harman (1984) with his claim that the rules of logic have no *special pertinence* for how we should reason. It is not our intention to get involved in this debate. Our focus is rather on how the perceived relationship between our logical theories and how we (should) reason has led to an unwanted equivocation in the epistemology of logic. We remain agnostic on whether, and to what extent, our theories of validity inform our reasoning. For more on the normativity of logic debate, see Steinberger (2020).

Marseille this weekend' on the basis of 'I'll either go to Herne Bay or Marseille this weekend' and 'I won't go to Herne Bay again' is deemed *logical* because it's sanctioned by the (putatively valid) rule of disjunctive syllogism expressed by formal logics. This equivocation becomes stark when one speaks of '*logical inferences*', which can be used to refer equally to the *rules* of implication within a logic and *particular inferences* made within the natural language sanctioned by these rules. Thus, the adjective (and honorific) 'logical' has come to stand ambiguously for the *principles of logic* and the *instances of reasoning* to which these principles apply. This equivocation can have unfortunate consequences for the epistemology of logic.

1.2 Equating the Epistemology of Logic with that of 'Logical' Reasoning

One consequence of equating logic with the study of good reasoning is that discussions of the epistemology of *logic* slip easily into the epistemology of *good reasoning*. Specifying logic's epistemology just becomes specifying that of good reasoning: under what conditions an individual reasons reliably, logically speaking, or under what conditions an individual is justified in making (putatively logical) inferences. This has led to an insufficient differentiation being made between the requirements necessary to be justified in making a *particular* (putatively logical) *inference* and those necessary to be justified in *proposing a logic*. The epistemology of *logica artificialis* has become either equated with that of *logica naturalis* or disregarded as the cost of focusing on the latter.

An example of the former problem is illustrated in BonJour's (1998) case for the indispensability of rational intuition for epistemic justification. When it comes to logical justification, BonJour deals with the need for rational intuition to justify (logical) *inferences* and our beliefs regarding logical *laws* in one fell swoop. Rational intuition is required to explain our success in making inferences from sets of premises to a conclusion, for neither empirical justification nor analyticity can account for inferential justification (1998: 4–5). Yet, BonJour makes the exact same point about justification for certain logical *laws*, such as the law of non-contradiction (1998: 33–4). Our justification for these laws cannot plausibly come from empirical sources or analyticity; only rational insight will do the job. Thus, no differentiation is made between the epistemic requirements for *reasoning* (*logically*) and becoming justified in *believing logical laws*. Both are straightforwardly acquired through intuition.

In fact, BonJour moves freely between talking about the need for rational intuition to justify logical inferences and laws:

> [W]hen I carefully and reflectively consider the proposition (or inference) in question, I am able simply to see or grasp or apprehend that the proposition is *necessary*, that it must be true in any possible world or situation (or alternatively that the conclusion of the inference must be true if the premises are true). (1998: 106).

Yet, there's no reason to assume that the conditions under which we are justified in making inferences of a certain type must be the same as those determining when we are justified in believing the principles sanctioning those inferences. Of course, they *may* turn out to be the same, but failing to separate the two matters precludes us from adequately addressing the question.

On other occasions, interpreting the epistemology of *logic* as the epistemology of (successful) *reasoning* exemplifies itself as a total *omission* of how we justify our best logical theories, as with Schechter's (2010) attempt to provide a naturalistic explanation of 'ordinary thinker's' justification for logic in terms of natural selection.

For Schechter, the epistemology of logic 'has two main explanatory tasks – to explain how it is that our logical beliefs are reliable and to explain how it is that we are epistemically responsible in believing as we do' (2010: 438). Yet, while Schechter talks explicitly about logical *beliefs* rather than inferences, he is not concerned with how we come to determine the correct logical *laws* (that is, with matters of *logica artificialis*). Rather, he is concerned with how individuals come to reliably deduce and, as a result, believe everyday natural-language claims, such as 'Every walrus is a walrus', which are deemed *logically* true by the correct logic (whatever logic that ultimately is). In other words, Schechter is concerned exclusively with the reliability of *logica naturalis*. Here, the epistemology of logic's main tasks is conceived so as to focus exclusively on the reliability of *logica naturalis,* omitting any consideration of how we come to be justified in believing the correct logic that sanctions these inferential practices.

A more complex and instructive example is Maddy's (2007) alternative naturalistic account of logic, which is simultaneously a metaphysical project providing an account of what *grounds* logical facts, and a theory of how we come to reliably believe the resulting logical truths (2007: 199). In both cases, consistent with naturalistic principles, Maddy intends to work from 'within science', using its methods and best current theories.

Maddy's answer to the metaphysical question is that logical facts are grounded in the *structural features* of the world. Specifically, our world exhibits a KF-structure (short for *Kant-Frege* structure), meaning that it 'consists of a domain of objects that bear properties and stand in relations, perhaps some universal properties, plus compounds of these involving conjunctions, disjunctions and negations, and [that] some interconnections between these situations are robust ground-consequent dependencies' (2007: 228). What results from these KF-structures is the truth of a 'rudimentary logic', with similarities to the truth-value gappy strong Kleene logic (**K3**). The epistemological question is then answered by proposing that individuals are suitably sensitive to these logical facts in virtue of their cognitive apparatus allowing them to 'detect and represent' these structural features of the world (2007: Sect. 3.5).[5]

The overall picture is bold and attractive. It provides an account of logic that maintains its objectivity without appealing to a Platonic third realm. Yet, there is an ambiguity in Maddy's work over the subject of this 'logical' justification, which impacts the resulting epistemology. Does this sensitivity to the logical facts provide us with the *laws* of logic constituting our best logical theories, or simply allow individuals to adopt *reliable inferential practices* that deliver them with beliefs which happen to be (logically) true? In other words, is Maddy concerned with providing an epistemology of *logica artificialis*, or an account of the reliability of *logica naturalis*?

At times, Maddy is clear it's the latter: '[t]he logical truths I have in mind are the simplest, most uncontroversial examples', such as 'If all oaks are trees and this is an oak, then this must be a tree' (2007: 199). Rather than logical *laws*, then, Maddy is concerned with how individuals come to reliably form (logically correct) beliefs, like Schechter.

Yet, at the same time, Maddy *also* seems concerned with explaining how, given that rudimentary logic is true of our world, we came to endorse classical logic (2007: Sect. III.7). A question which has nothing to do with the reliability of *logica naturalis*, but rather with what justifies our endorsement of our best logical *theory* (presumed to be classical logic). Maddy's proposal is that classical logic is an idealisation of rudimentary logic, arrived at by presuming each predicate has a sharp boundary, all names refer, and that the conditional behaves truth-functionally rather than representing causality.[6]

Clearly, we've now moved on to the distinct epistemological question of what justifies our endorsement of a particular logic; an epistemology of *logica artificialis*. Yet, as an epistemology of *logica artificialis*, it is insufficient. We are not provided with details of how we went about discovering and ultimately became justified in believing this (idealised) theory of the logical facts. What is it that justifies our endorsement of classical logic, rather than, say, a constructivist logic?

---

[5] We're passing over some unnecessary complications here. For instance, due to findings from quantum mechanics, Maddy (2007: 247–57) eventually concludes that while the world isn't actually constituted of KF-structures, the macro-world *behaves as though* it is and *appears* to be to us humans, which is enough to explain our reliability with regards to (logical) reasoning.

[6] For more on the role of idealisation in logical theorising, see Russell (2023).

The answer cannot simply be that classical logic is a faithful, if idealised, representation of the logical facts delivered by the structures of our KF-world. This simply tells us what makes classical logic (idealisations aside) *true*, not how we came to be *justified* in believing it. The fact that Avogadro's law accurately reflects facts about the nature of gases is not what justifies our commitment to the law. This might explain what makes it *true*, but not how we came to be justified in believing the law in the first place.

At one point, Maddy appears to explain our justification for endorsing classical logic on the basis of it being an idealisation of rudimentary logic, which is not only 'true of the world' but also 'embedded in our most primitive modes of cognition and representation' (2007: 288). However, putting aside the point that classical logic is supposed to be an *idealisation* of the logical facts, a process which requires complex theorising, the fact that certain principles are embedded within our 'modes of cognition and representation' will not suffice to explain how we became justified in believing a theory expressing these principles. After all, while the grammatical rules of my mother tongue may be embedded within my Broca's area, this does not mean these rules are luminous to me. In fact, it's implausible that they are. Otherwise, we would not need descriptive linguistics to discover these rules; we could simply ask native speakers directly what the grammatical rules are.

Thus, even if we admit that the fact these principles of rudimentary logic are embedded within our modes of cognition (partially) explains how we come to make reliable (logical) inferences about the world, it does not explain how we became justified in believing what these principles are. In general, being *sensitive* to a set of facts or rules determining competent practice, ensuring compliance with them, does not ensure one has conscious access to these facts or constitutive rules.

In particular, if sensitivity to the logical facts were enough to be justified in believing them, it would make sense to say that skilled mathematicians were justified in believing the principles of first- (or second-) order classical logic prior to the twentieth century because they exhibited the ability to reason in accordance with them within their proofs. Yet, they were not. For this, we required the ingenuity of Frege, Russell, and Whitehead. Whenever there is a body of principles related to the competent performance of individuals on a task, the epistemology of the correct principles dictating that practice is distinct from the epistemic conditions of the competent practice itself. This is true of language use, it is true of arithmetic, and it is true of logic. A speaker of English can be well aware that the sentence 'The black huge dog' sounds wrong while 'The huge black dog' sounds fine, without knowing *why*. Similarly, competency in inference does not entail reflective awareness of the (logical) laws constituting this competency.

These brief examples highlight the dangers of inadequately distinguishing between an epistemology of *good logical reasoning* (competent *logica naturalis*) and logical theorising (*logica artificialis*). It can lead us to either completely omitting consideration of the latter or presuming that an answer to the latter straightforwardly follows from the former. We now advance our point further, showing that there are (at least) five distinct levels of 'logical' justification, each increasing in sophistication and understanding over the last; some concerned with being a reliable reasoner, others with gaining justification for the correct logical principles. Given that the conditions for possessing each level are distinct, this further shows the need to distinguish an epistemology of *logica artificialis* from the epistemic requirements to be a reliable (logical) reasoner.

1.3 Five 'Levels' of Logical Justification

Level 1: Logical Competency. *Reliably making (logical) inferences.*

At the most rudimentary level of logical justification is the ability to reliably infer *in accordance* with those standards deemed logical. The individual possessing this justification can reason their way from 'I'll have to pay a fine if I don't pay for parking' and 'I don't want to get fined' to the conclusion that they better pay for parking. What is not required for this level of justification is a conscious propositional belief that these relevant inferences are good (let alone *valid*). Nor is there a requirement that the individual is sensitive to any distinction between logical and non-logical inferences, assuming there is one. This form of (logical) justification is akin to the linguistic competence we expect of native speakers. Their justification consists in being able to *competently engage* in a practice sanctioned by a set of tacit rules.

Due to the purely practical nature of this form of justification, without any associated conscious beliefs, some may hesitate to call this justification at all, but merely *competence*. Indeed, as there is no requirement that the agent has access to the reasons *why* the relevant inferences are acceptable, it is more appropriate to call this level of logical justification an instance of *warrant* rather than justification in the technical sense. As with linguistic competency, our agent is said to possess warrant for these inferential activities by virtue of their reliability in making such inferences in accordance with the correct laws of implication.[7]

---

[7] What *explains* this reliability, and what constitutes reasoning *in accordance with* the correct laws are of course the pressing questions for any epistemology of *logica naturalis*.

The exact requirements for this rudimentary form of warrant are a live topic in the epistemology of reasoning. After all, not just any mental transition from one cognitive state to another is usually deemed an *inference*. A standing belief of mine can merely cause me to form a new belief, by loose association or programmed conditioning, and we would usually wish to distinguish such cases from those in which one infers a new belief *on the basis of* others. One common means to differentiate mere mental movements from inferences is to require that the movement in the latter case is caused by an associated recognition that the standing beliefs *support* the new belief, which Boghossian (2014) calls the *taking condition*:

> For some R to constitute an inference in some doxastic circumstance C, then one's R-ing must in part be explained by one's taking some elements of C to justify one's R-ing.

Determining whether fulfilling the *taking condition* or something similar is required to count as making a (logical) inference is unnecessary for our purposes.[8] We are not concerned with providing a fully-fledged epistemology of *reasoning*. All we require is that, firstly, being able to reliably make a logical inference does not entail that one is justified in believing the principles determining this reliability and, secondly, that fulfilling the *taking condition* does not require a conscious attitude towards those arguments representing the inferences being made. The first requirement is clearly fulfilled by most reliable reasoners, and the second by reasoners who lack the desire or capacity to consciously reflect on their inferential practice (including children).

Level 2: Conscious Good Practice. *Justified belief that some propositions follow from others.*

This brings us to the second 'level' of logical justification, *Conscious Good Practice,* which requires an agent to have conscious attitudes towards the relevant set of propositions. This level of justification is achieved by an agent in virtue of, firstly, consciously reflecting on their inferential activities, such that they not only *take* some standing doxastic states to support a new one but deem the associated argument representing the inference to be *good*. Second, they appreciate that the associated argument is not simply *good*, but that those propositions expressing the standing beliefs (the premises) *guarantee* the proposition expressing the new belief (the conclusion). In other words, they can reliably differentiate between arguments in which the premises

---

[8] For the relevant debate, see Hlobil (2014) and McHugh & Way (2016).

merely lend *support* to the conclusion and those in which the premises *guarantee* it.

Yet, while there's sensitivity here to the distinction between *deductively* and *non*-deductively good arguments, there is none to the differentiation between logical and *non*-logical inferences, nor to whether an argument is good for *logical* reasons. Thus, our individual possessing *Conscious Good Practice* has no way to differentiate the implication from 'I'll be late to work if my car breaks down' and 'my car's broken down' to 'I'll be late for work', which is often considered a logical implication, and standard non-logical *lexical entailments* such as 'John was murdered', so 'John is dead'. In both cases, for our individual, the conclusion just seems to *follow from* the premise(s).

Indeed, while there's evidence from cognitive science that everyday reasoners can differentiate between non-deductive and deductive inferences (Goel et al. 1997), there is none to suggest that they possess a similar appreciation for the distinction between logical and non-logical deductive inferences. The latter only arises at more theoretical levels of understanding, when formal systems are constructed to explain the goodness of these inferences. Relatedly, at this level, there is no appreciation yet of *why* exactly these arguments are good; simply that they are. Explaining why an argument is good requires specifying the relevant considerations that differentiate good arguments from bad.

Level 3: Good Schema Justification. *Justified belief that some propositions follow from others, based upon structural features.*

Here we have not only the justified belief that an argument is good, but also some sensitivity to the *reasons why*; reasons commonly associated with logicality. Specifically, that there are certain *structural* features of the argument that explain its goodness. For instance, that the inference to 'I'll go to Marseille this weekend' on the basis of 'I'll either go to Herne Bay or Marseille this weekend' and 'I won't go to Herne Bay again' is good *because* it exemplifies the form 'Either P or Q, but not P, and so Q'. There may even be some awareness that these structural features are shared by multiple arguments, which are jointly acceptable in virtue of possessing them.

Recognition of this fact is the starting point of *formal* logic: that an argument is good *in virtue of its form* (in some sense). This level of logical justification is akin to the type of intuitive grammatical reflection common among language users when trying to make sense of their linguistic intuitions, prompted by a child's inquiry or a tricky case. For instance, that when using modal verbs in a question, the verb always comes before the subject ('Can I borrow this?' rather than 'I can borrow this?').[9] Such reflection presumes that even if the grammatical rules are not transparent to us, there are still, nonetheless, pertinent rules determining whether a sentence in the language is meaningful or not. Similarly, while we need not have the rules dictating acceptable inferential standards at hand, there is still, nonetheless, such a set of principles governing the correctness of our inferential activities.

While *Good Schema* justification distinguishes itself from the previous level in terms of its sensitivity towards some of the factors that make an argument good, there are still important elements missing that differentiate it from the level of theoretical understanding desired in contemporary logic.

First, the recognition that some arguments are good due to their structural features is not enough to differentiate logical from non-logical implications. After all, non-logical implications can exemplify a *lexical* structure that explains their validity. This differentiation between logical and non-logical considerations only occurs at a more theoretical level, when logical *connectives* are posited within a logic to explain why sets of arguments are good.

Second, there is no appreciation yet of *why* arguments of these forms are good. Rather, all we have are generalisations over arguments in the form of schemata, arrived at through abstraction from specific arguments deemed acceptable. Yet, generalisations need not themselves constitute explanations. The generalisation 'All swans are white' does not tell us *why* swans are that colour, only that they are.

Similarly, identifying that arguments of a given form are good need not tell us why exemplifying this form makes them good – simply that they are. I can appreciate that every argument of the form 'Either P or Q, but not P, and so Q' is good, without having an idea as to *why*. Specifically, I might not be able to explain why arguments of this form are good, but the same can't be said of arguments of the form 'P if Q, P, and so Q'.

Of course, this doesn't mean that an insight into the structural features of arguments is worthless. There is an important distinction to be made between *predictively useful* heuristics and genuinely *explanatory* models. Being aware of these structural features through abstraction can successfully regulate our inferential activities and attitudes towards arguments to an extent, and so have predictive value, without explaining *why* the arguments are good.

For related reasons, there is no recognition yet that these arguments are *valid*. Validity is a technical concept posited by our logical theories to explain *why* an

---

[9] Like many generalisations about grammar, this rule is false. There are multiple contexts in which English speakers would put the subject before the modal verb. For instance, the rhetorical 'You can cook?' is perfectly acceptable. Reflections on the 'good' schematic form of arguments can similarly lead us astray.

argument is good, whether in model-theoretic, proof-theoretic, or other terms. Effective use of the concept requires going beyond a mere recognition that arguments are good due to their structural features; it requires us to be able to explain what differentiates those forms which are good from those which are not. This brings us to a final difference between *Good Schema* justification and deeper theoretical levels. The intuitive principles being drawn about 'good' forms of argument at this level are still formulated within a regimented quasi-natural language, not in the precisely defined artificial languages of modern logic. Thus, understanding the schemata determining the intuitive goodness of the arguments *presupposes* an understanding of the existing object language, and so the natural-language arguments instantiating these forms.

This means that using these schemata to show that a given argument is good will suffer from those concerns historically raised against syllogistic logic. Unless there are failures of memory, or the particular argument is difficult to parse, being informed of the 'good' schematised principle will tell one nothing that one could not have already appreciated by just looking at the specific argument. If one does not already see that 'I'll go to Marseille this weekend' follows from 'I'll either go to Herne Bay or Marseille this weekend' and 'I won't go to Herne Bay again', one will hardly be convinced by being told that it is an instance of 'Either P or Q, but not P, and so Q'. After all, to appreciate that exemplifying this schema suffices for the argument being good requires one to recognise the goodness of the specific arguments (putatively) instantiating the schema in the first place. The schematisation is just a universal generalisation over the argument instances; either I already accepted the argument was good, or I'll have my doubts about the purportedly 'good schema'. The possibility of being able to explain *why* sentences of the object language entail others, without presupposing an understanding of the arguments, will need to wait until a formal language with its own semantics is constructed.

Thus, while the agent possessing *Good Schema* justification possesses a degree of reflection about their inferential activities (*logica naturalis*), and thus a level of regulated mastery of such inferences not found at prior levels, it falls short of the justification we strive for in contemporary logic.

Level 4: Logical Laws Justification. *Justified belief that some logical rules are valid.*

We now move to the level of theoretical justification one gains from taking an introductory logic or discrete mathematics course. Here, the agent has an understanding of the basic presupposition of formal logic – that there are underlying structures which determine an argument's validity – an appreciation of the pertinent formal languages (whether propositional, first-order, or higher), the distinction between logical and non-logical vocabulary, and the concept VALIDITY.

Further, they will have learnt some of the logical rules, such as *modus ponens*, disjunctive syllogism, and reductio, which play an important role within our inferential practices. If pushed, they may even be able to provide a proof of the validity of an argument using the tools given to them, whether truth-tables, model theory, or natural deduction. In this sense, they can be said to be capable of providing a rudimentary form of *explanation* as to why a specific natural-language argument is valid: when suitably formalised, there is a proof of the conclusion from its premises using only the acceptable rules of the logic, and so on.

What is still missing, however, is an appreciation of *why* these formal rules are the rules that dictate validity rather than others, *why* validity is defined in just this fashion rather than another, and *why* this specific formal language is used rather than others. In other words, what is lacking is an appreciation of what justifies the theoretical postulates being taught to them in the first place.

Level 5: Theory-Choice Justification. *Justified belief that some logic $\mathcal{L}$ is the correct logic of validity.*

This brings us to the deepest level of logical justification, where the agent is justified in believing that a particular logic is true. Here, the justification possessed goes beyond that of the previous level in virtue of an awareness of what justifies the choice of logic: why, for instance, we should embrace a logic that validates disjunctive syllogism, why we should use a first-order language rather than a higher-order language, and so on.

Being aware of what justifies a choice of logic requires the agent to have some sensitivity to what constitutes suitable evidence for a logic. Just as a scientist who is aware of what justifies the choice between competing theories must have sensitivity to what constitutes suitable evidence for these theories. This does not mean, of course, that the individual has a detailed *reflective understanding* of what constitutes evidence for a logic; it simply means that they are sensitive to these reasons. Possessing a full-blown reflective understanding of the methodology of these decisions is something we only expect at the level of the *philosophy of* logic.

Notice that, other than through testimony, many philosophers won't possess justification of this kind. That is, being capable of explaining *why* classical logic is better than intuitionistic or a relevant logic, for instance, or *why* we should define validity in model-theoretic rather than proof-theoretic terms. Indeed, the defining feature of *Theory-Choice* justification, that the agent has access to the reasons why it is rational to endorse a particular logic over others, ensures that *within* this level there will be infinite gradations of justification. One could be aware of the arguments for classical logic while unaware of those weaknesses highlighted by non-classical research programmes. Further, one might be aware of the challenges posed by intuitionistic logic but not by substructural logics, and so on. In this respect, possessing *Theory-Choice* justification within logic is no different from that within the sciences; the extent to which one possesses this level of justification will depend upon one's expertise and experience in the field.

Importantly, gaining this level of justification requires more than being informed about the current 'textbook logic'. One must engage in logical research. Only then can one understand why certain theoretical choices are better than others, and why some logics are preferable to others. It is achieving this level of understanding and justification which constitutes an aim of contemporary logic. Thus, appreciating *how* logicians gain this level of understanding can properly be considered one of the aims of an epistemology of *logica artificialis*.

1.4 The Epistemology of Logica Artificialis

Clearly, then, one can possess *Logical Competency* without *Theory-Choice* justification. Most individuals will be reliable reasoners without ever becoming justified in believing that *modus ponens* is valid, let alone that classical logic is correct. Logical (reasoning) competency is not peculiar in this regard. It is normal to be competent in a practice without being justified in believing the principles determining this competency. One can be quite adept at arithmetic without knowing anything whatsoever about the axioms of Peano arithmetic.

Consequently, understanding the conditions under which someone becomes a competent practitioner is distinct from understanding how an individual gains epistemic access to those principles dictating competency. Specifically, an epistemology of reliable (logical) inference won't directly provide us with insight into how we become justified in believing a logic (*logica artificialis*). Mere sensitivity to the logical facts (if there are any) does not suffice to explain how we came to construct and test those (logical) theories we now accept, nor how we demonstrated them to be better than competitors.

Thus, even if, ultimately, the value of *logica artificialis* lies in its ability to elucidate those rules properly regulating *logica naturalis*, determining the epistemology of *logica artificialis* is not equivalent to determining the conditions for reliable (logical) reasoning. Granted, then, that providing an epistemology of reliable (logical) *reasoning* doesn't suffice for an epistemology of logical *theorising*. But why care about the latter? Why strive for an epistemology of *logica artificialis*?

We do not only consider ourselves to be reliable reasoners. We construct logics to demonstrate why certain claims follow others, and in doing so, we take ourselves to be sanctioning many of the inferences that mathematicians and scientists rely upon. However, presumably, we don't believe that our choice of logic is arbitrary; some theories are better than others. Classical logicians rarely admit that their choice of logic is based on personal taste. What justifies their conclusion? Why think that we are rationally justified in endorsing a specific logic, and that some logic $\mathcal{L}_1$ is better than another $\mathcal{L}_2$? Only an adequate epistemology of *logica artificialis* can provide an answer.

Further, these questions are intimately tied to other important topics within the philosophy of logic, such as the extent to which logic's epistemology is similar to that of the recognised sciences (Williamson 2007), and whether, unlike disagreements in other areas of inquiry, disagreements about logic are inherently irrational (Martin 2021c). Again, only an epistemology of *logica artificialis* can address these matters.

Nor should an informative epistemology of *logica artificialis* only help in understanding the past. Yes, it should help us appreciate why it was rational to move from syllogistic to classical logic, say. But it may also help us understand how we can *improve* our theories in the future. By understanding more precisely the criteria for a successful logic, we should be able to appreciate more fully those opportunities for improving upon our current theories. Just as in the sciences, we should believe that a more methodologically *reflective* practitioner in logic is a more *effective* practitioner.

These considerations show that there are significant benefits to possessing an epistemology of *logica artificialis*, which could not be achieved through an epistemology of good (logical) reasoning alone. At present, however, these are just bold promises, an electoral manifesto. Delivering upon them requires that we use the correct philosophical method to investigate *logica artificialis*. Failure to use an appropriate methodology is a further reason we have yet to possess a fully fledged epistemology of logic, unlike for the sciences. How we should go about engaging in the epistemology of *logica artificialis* is the topic of the next section.

2 The Practice-Based Approach

In the previous section, we argued that it would be a mistake to assimilate the epistemology of logic with that of good reasoning. Fully understanding logic's epistemology requires moving beyond questions of what constitutes our justification for making specific (logical) inferences to what justifies our choice of logic and claims about these logics. Our next question, then, is: How do we go about this epistemology of *logica artificialis*? Here, we are concerned with philosophical *methodology*; what method should philosophers use to discover the epistemology of some domain?

When attempting to understand the epistemology of a domain, whether it be mathematical, scientific, or everyday perceptual knowledge, there can be a temptation to be led by what we *expect* knowledge of this type to be like or which properties knowledge within this domain *should* possess. Further, we can be driven by the desire to solve specific epistemic puzzles regarding these types of knowledge, brought about by general sceptical concerns or our own philosophical commitments. In these cases, the goal is to provide an epistemology of the domain that respects those properties we wish to assign to it while avoiding perceived unsavoury consequences.

Such an approach has historically been common within the philosophy of science. Popper's (1959) rejection of verificationism and advocacy of falsificationism were motivated not on the basis of conclusions drawn from detailed case studies of scientific theory-choice, but by perceived threats to scientific knowledge. First, that there were theories portraying themselves as scientific but which fell short of the standards required to be properly scientific. Given that permitting these pseudo-scientific theories the same status as the sciences could have negative societal consequences, it was important that they were clearly discriminated. This was a requirement verificationism could not fulfil, given that it is all too easy to find favourable evidence for any theory, scientifically proper or not. Second, only falsificationism (putatively) could avoid the use of inductive inferences within the scientific enterprise, and thus the sceptical conclusions following from Hume's problem.

A similar story can be told for some epistemologies of mathematics. Katz's (1998) rationalist account of mathematical justification in terms of intuition is motivated not by a detailed consideration of the forms of evidence mathematicians provide for their claims, but a desire to explain how knowledge about mathematics is *possible* while maintaining a commitment to realism about abstract mathematical objects.[10] The commitment to abstract mathematical objects itself having been motivated by a dissatisfaction with anti-realist alternatives.

These proposals exemplify a *top-down* approach to the epistemology of a domain. One begins with certain success criteria for what the epistemology of

---

[10] This challenge of explaining our reliable epistemic access to non-spatiotemporal facts is sometimes known as the *Benacerraf-Field problem* (Benacerraf 1973; Field 1989).

the domain *should* look like. These may include avoiding a particular sceptical challenge, respecting the author's own expectations regarding the metaphysics of the area, complying with specific established epistemological assumptions about rationality, or conforming to historical precedents concerning the domain. From these background motivations and commitments, one then attempts to infer an epistemology of the domain that respects these restrictions. Thus, respecting the restrictions becomes one of, if not *the* primary, success conditions for an account of the epistemology of the domain. Giving these philosophical criteria methodological and evidential primacy is what makes the approach *top-down*.

A *top-down* approach is not our only option, however. Rather than beginning with standing assumptions about the specific area of knowledge, we can begin with putative instances of good epistemic practice within the relevant domain. From these instances, we can then slowly construct an account of the epistemology of the domain, testing these proposals against more and more novel cases until we find a proposal that coheres with the available cases. In other words, a *bottom-up* approach. Given that this approach studies the epistemology of a domain by looking at the activities of its practitioners, it is also commonly known as a *practice-based approach* (Dutilh Novaes 2012; Martin 2022).

While the practice-based approach is well-established within the philosophies of science and mathematics, the same is not true of the philosophy of logic. As we shall see, it is still common within the epistemology of logic to find arguments for proposals based upon their ability to avoid sceptical consequences while respecting the authors' own favoured philosophical presumptions. What results from this focus on meeting predetermined philosophical criteria, however, are accounts of logic's epistemology that tend to oversimplify the processes involved in the justification of logics while problematising the actual practices of logicians. The result being that use of a top-down approach is another common cause of our lack of progress in understanding logic's epistemology.

The goal of this section is to highlight the benefits of a practice-based approach to the epistemology of logic. If we desire a detailed account of logic's epistemology, we are best off looking at *what logicians actually do*. Our justification for this claim takes two forms. First, we show the advantages that the approach has provided for our understanding of the epistemology of the sciences and mathematics. By analogy, given that *logica artificialis* is a research area just as the sciences are, it would be a surprise if the approach didn't offer our understanding of logic's epistemology similar benefits. We then argue more directly for the approach when it comes to logic's epistemology, by showing that top-down approaches have had negative consequences in the philosophy of logic, focusing on Quine's defence of evidential holism. These arguments are then treated as a springboard for our more general case for a practice-based approach in the sections that follow, in which we use the approach to deliver an informative epistemology of *logica artificialis*. In this sense, as with most methods, the proof of the pudding will be in the eating.

Given that our initial motivation for a practice-based approach to the epistemology of logic comes from its prior successes in the philosophies of science and mathematics, it makes sense to begin there.

2.1 Motivation for the Practice-Based Approach

The practice-based approach is defined, firstly, by its dissatisfaction with top-down approaches and, secondly, its proposal for how to rectify these shortcomings. It first emerged in the 1960s in response to perceived inadequacies with traditional philosophical approaches towards the sciences (Soler et al. 2014), which were criticised for producing accounts that were:

(i) *too idealised*, being based upon a priori reflections of what we *want* the sciences to look like, or what they *should* look like given our preconceptions, rather than reflecting the reality of scientific research;
(ii) *over simplistic*, in failing to reflect the plurality of aims and methods within science;
(iii) *too present-centred*, falling foul of a tendency to produce Whig histories by presuming science's history is a story of smooth and unstoppable progress up to the present state of affairs; and
(iv) *too end-product focused*, focusing on the properties of theories and neglecting the processes that led to the discovery of these results.

An early example of these concerns is found in Kuhn's (1962) criticisms of Popper's (1959) falsificationism, which is denounced for both idealising scientific methodology by presenting a naïve picture of scientific progress as a continual chain of evermore informative theories that perpetually become falsified, and for being too present-centred by presuming that the aims and norms for the evaluation of past scientific theories were the same as those of contemporary science. Further, Kuhn criticised previous accounts of scientific methodology for paying too little attention to the rich variety of activities constituting the actual scientific method, such as the designing and testing of experimental equipment and their use in measuring constants, rather than simply testing hypotheses.

Around the start of the twenty-first century, similar practice-based research began in the philosophy of mathematics, with traditional approaches being criticised for possessing too idealised a picture of mathematics (Corfield 2003). The most prominent of these concerns was the long-standing claim that mathematical knowledge is comprised wholly of theorems evidenced by formal proofs. Contrary to this view, it was argued that if one looks at mathematical practice, understanding progresses in many ways, including through informal proofs whose positive epistemic qualities are *irreducible* to those of formal proofs (Larvor 2012). Further, similar to how top-down approaches were criticised for missing significant elements of the scientific method, practice-based philosophers of mathematics criticised traditional philosophy of mathematics for neglecting important features of the enterprise, including the appraisal of definitions (Tappenden 2008) and the use of diagrams (Giardino 2017).

Thus, we can see *two* distinct motivations for the approach. First, its ability to provide more *accurate* accounts of how epistemology in the research area proceeds, ensuring our philosophical proposals do not lead to swathes of activities in the field being deemed epistemically inappropriate. This, of course, is what ultimately happened with Popper's falsificationism, which denied probabilistic and existential claims the status of being properly scientific.

Second, the approach is able to provide a more *comprehensive* understanding of the field's epistemology by bringing to light features of its methodology neglected by top-down approaches. After all, we cannot expect a theory starting from first principles to appreciate all of the important procedures constituting a research field's methodology, any more than we can expect to understand the methods of a master carpenter or high court judge from first principles. We must look at what they do.

It is here that the approach has had significant, often unsung, successes. For instance, the recognition of the role of model-building in the sciences is a paradigm example of how our understanding of scientific methodology has significantly improved by looking at the practices of scientists. Not only do we now have a fine understanding of the various purposes and types of scientific models, but we also have detailed accounts of the various virtues that sub-fields of science value in their models (Weisberg 2013). None of this would have been possible without looking in detail at the activities of scientists.

Both of the approach's benefits are a result of attempts to rectify perceived failures of traditional top-down approaches. First, by reorienting our *aims* when providing a philosophical account of a field's epistemology. Rather than attempting to construct grand unified theories of the essential nature of the sciences or mathematics conforming to our preconceptions of their purposes, subject-matter, or epistemology, we should aim to produce an understanding of these human endeavours that: (i) reflects the reality of research within them; (ii) recognises the plurality of aims and methods found across them; (iii) situates results within their proper historical context; (iv) recognises the development of the field's methodological norms; and (v) gives equal attention to the processes of discovery as to the properties of the eventual products (Soler et al. 2014).

Second, by selecting appropriate methods to meet these aims. Specifically, four methodological norms are important in differentiating the practice-based approach from its top-down siblings. *First*, the most reliable guide we have to the epistemology of a field is the activities of its practitioners. Thus, more time should be spent looking at how scientists and mathematicians go about achieving their research goals than ruminating on the nature of science or what constitutes a mathematical object. This does not mean one's inquiry cannot be prompted by philosophical presumptions or puzzles. But, to be reliably tested, proposals must ultimately face the tribunal of actual practice in the research area. Analogously, while it's perfectly acceptable for scientific hypotheses to be motivated by a whole host of considerations, they must eventually stand up to rigorous empirical testing. Understandably, much of this work will take the form of case studies, whether in-depth studies of the activities of particular researchers or research teams, or wider studies of the norms within specific sub-fields. However, it can also take the form of historiographic studies looking at the development of techniques or concepts within a field.[11]

Second, when there is a clash between prominent practices in the field and background philosophical assumptions, *evidential priority* is given to practices within the field. This is because how experts go about justifying their theories is a more reliable guide to the aims, methods, and epistemology of the research area than our philosophical presuppositions; therefore, the former should (in most cases) be given a higher credence.[12]

Third, we should be wary of making exceptionless generalisations that go beyond particular sub-fields, research programmes, or time-periods unless justified by the data. This is a corollary of using case studies of actual practice as one's primary data. As with any empirical inquiry, one should be hesitant, first, to extrapolate too much beyond one's sample until similar results have been found elsewhere and, second, to presume that the same findings will hold when notable variables are altered, such as time-period and sub-field. It may, of course, turn out that what we discover for one time-period or research

---

[11] For more on the various types of studies and data used within the practice-based approach, see Hamami & Morris (2020).

[12] Why only in *most* cases? This is not the empty caveat it may seem. We must be open to the possibility that individual members of the community make mistakes and so do not reflect the general methodological norms of the field. Thus, as with any empirical finding, we shouldn't be too hasty in drawing dramatic conclusions from individual cases. This concern can be addressed through considering a range of case studies and identifying outliers.

programme holds for others, but this conclusion needs to be substantiated by *actually looking at* these cases too. Importantly, nothing stops the philosopher using a practice-based approach from putting forward bold generalisations about a field's epistemology. Indeed, for our proposals to have any predictive power, they must go beyond those cases considered so far. However, these generalisations should be treated as tentative and requiring further testing against suitable new cases.

Lastly, we should be open to exploring features of the field's methods beyond those traditionally taken seriously by philosophers. This does not mean that *every* activity practitioners perform within their research will be of philosophical interest, but we should not constrain ourselves to just traditional philosophical questions (interesting though they are). It is this feature of the approach that has allowed it to motivate novel and fruitful research questions about the sciences that were previously neglected, including studies into model-building, the uses of computer-aided proofs (Avigad 2008), and the relationship of simulations to experimentation (Winsberg 2019).

What, though, do these prior successes of the approach tell us about its prospects within the philosophy of logic, and the epistemology of logic in particular? Firstly, they provide us with *prima facie* evidence that the same benefits will apply to the philosophy of logic, especially when it comes to the epistemology of *logica artificialis*. After all, *logica artificialis* is a field of research with its own aims and methods, like the sciences. Further, its activities are performed by experienced practitioners who have demonstrable expertise. This already lends support to the conclusion that the approach will be a more reliable method to inform our epistemology of logic than top-down approaches.

However, we can also be more direct in our support for the approach. Firstly, by highlighting examples in which top-down approaches have led to similar problems in the epistemology of logic as in the philosophies of science and mathematics, and secondly, by demonstrating how the practice-based approach can help avoid these problems. As one would expect, this latter aim is best realised by showing what the approach can achieve. We begin with the case for raising similar concerns against top-down approaches within the philosophy of logic.

2.2 Top-Down Approaches in the Philosophy of Logic

Top-down approaches are common within the philosophy of logic. Kneale (1956: 238) rejects the possibility of domain-specific logics, for then 'logic' would simply become 'a name for any collection of rules in accordance with which we may argue in some context'. Logical laws are, *by definition*, wholly general. Beall and Restall (2006: 91), on the other hand, require any *genuine* logic to have a transitive and reflexive consequence relation, despite there being well-developed research programmes proposing logics rejecting transitivity (Tennant 1987) and reflexivity (Martin and Meyer 1982). In each case, particular logical practices or products are considered unviable for contravening philosophical expectations about logic, regardless of whether these practices are taken seriously in the field or not.

However, it isn't simply that top-down approaches are used within the philosophy of logic. There's good reason to think that the concerns raised against top-down approaches in the philosophy of science are also pertinent in the philosophy of logic, impacting our understanding of the aims, epistemology, and wider methodology of logic.

Take, for instance, the tendency of top-down approaches to come to hasty generalisations, resulting in an unjustified *synchronically homogeneous* picture of the field.[13] As we saw in the previous section, there is a prominent presumption in the literature that there is some *canonical purpose* for logic, understood as the 'analysis of reasoning' (Priest 2006a: 196) or 'codification of logical consequence in natural language' (Cook 2010: 495). Yet, what justifies this presumption for contemporary logic is unclear.

Historically, *logica artificialis* was indeed intimately connected to *logica naturalis*. However, this in itself is not enough to determine the primary purpose of formal logic *now*, nor indeed that there is such a purpose. Short of a straightforward philosophical presumption, the only justification we find is appeals to logic's history. Cook (2010), for instance, attempts to justify his claim based upon the views of founding figures, such as Aristotle and Tarski. Yet Aristotle also suggested that science ought to aim at providing teleological explanations, and few scientists now take this activity seriously. In general, appealing to the views of the founding figures of a research area to establish its essence is to fall foul of the *embryonic* fallacy – the presumption that an activity has the same aims and purposes as when it was initially developed – and would equally require us to admit that the primary purpose of astronomy is to provide planetary data for the higher art of astrology.

Just as the theories and techniques in a field change over time, so can its aims. The development of symbolic logic, and later model and proof theory, opened new avenues of research and uses of logic that neither Aristotle nor (even) Tarski could foresee. To remain focused on those uses of logic which had primacy within its history is to neglect the changes in research priorities that

---

[13] For a more systematic account of the ways in which top-down approaches to the philosophy of logic suffer similar weaknesses to those in the philosophies of science and mathematics, see Martin (2022).

have occurred and the theoretical progress made. It is akin to suggesting that the primary aim of modern physics is to explain the behaviour of bodies within mechanistic terms because this is how Newton and Descartes conceived of the enterprise.

An unfortunate result of specifying a particular purpose of logic as *philosophically primary,* based upon precedent, is that other aims and uses of logic tend to be cast off as unworthy of philosophical study. Eklund (2020), for instance, claims that any form of logical pluralism not focused on the canonical or (philosophically) primary purpose of logic would be uninteresting. The implication is that it's not particularly philosophically interesting that we've been able to construct various logical systems differentially suited to modelling a range of phenomena or achieving varying goals. Yet, this not only downplays the significant technological innovations required to produce these results but is also deeply anachronistic. There was nothing inevitable about the development of linear logic or its fruitful application in understanding the grammaticality of languages.

It can also lead us to miss opportunities to address important questions about logic, such as the putative similarities between its methodology and that of the sciences. Scientific models are often fruitfully transferred from one science to another to model a range of phenomena (Tieleman 2022); epidemiological models, for instance, are applicable not only to infectious diseases but also to other infectious behaviours, such as civil disobedience. Yet the same is true of the mathematical structures produced by logic. Formal systems, which were initially proposed to solve one problem, have later been fruitfully applied to others. Kripke frames are now not only used to provide semantics for alethic modal logics but also to model deontic implications and doxastic phenomena. Type theory went from being a means to avoid unsavoury paradoxical results to being used to model legal reasoning (Benzmüller et al. 2020), and Łukasiewicz introduced many-valued logics to understand modalities, but now three-valued logics are used to model the states of frictional systems to solve Painlevé's paradox in rigid-body dynamics (Nosonovsky and Breki 2019).

While we may now take these applications of logic as a given, it was by no means inevitable that logic would evolve into a discipline with such a rich variety of systems with extensive applications. Focusing on a particular purpose of logic as the only 'philosophically' interesting one will inevitably lead us to having a poorer understanding of logic, missing many of the technological breakthroughs and subsequent 'scientific' progress it has achieved. Achievements which, to a large extent, are demonstrated by the ever-widening applicability of these systems and the ability of logicians to design systems with the intent purpose of fulfilling specific theoretical goals.

It is clear, then, that a top-down approach can lead to a more impoverished understanding of logic as an area of knowledge than is necessary. In comparison, a practice-based approach, which pays closer attention to the activities of researchers in the field, can allow us to appreciate these successes and understand the field's methodological norms, including their similarity to those of the recognised sciences.

Particularly relevant to us here is another weakness with top-down approaches, common among proposals in the epistemology of logic: producing *over-idealised* accounts of how we come to be justified in believing logical laws or theories, with the consequence of distorting our understanding of how logics are justified. In the next section, we show how foundationalist accounts of logic, which propose that we have some unmediated access to the laws of logic, distort the means through which logics are justified. Here, though, we focus on a *non-foundationalist* epistemology of logic, which is similarly motivated by top-down considerations and falls foul of the same problems: Quine's evidential holism.

2.3 Quine's Evidential Holism

Unlike foundationalist epistemologies of logic, non-foundationalist epistemologies propose that the correct laws of logic must be *inferred* and justified based upon other evidence or commitments we possess. One of the most historically prominent non-foundationalist epistemologies of logic is Quine's (1951) *evidential holism*, which claims that our logical commitments are justified as part of our wider web of belief and evaluated in light of the same evidence as theories within the natural sciences.

Quine's proposal has three main motivations. First, a deep dissatisfaction with existing foundationalist epistemologies of logic. Prior to Quine's proposal, there was a general assumption that one gained direct access to the truths of logic either through intuition or epistemic analyticity. Due to his own naturalistic propensities, Quine didn't take seriously the viability of a quasi-perceptual mental faculty like intuition; we should rely only upon those epistemic sources for which we have scientific support (1990: 19). Unlike other empiricists, however, Quine (1951, 1976) was also famously unmoved by the suggestion that we could explain our justification for logical laws in terms of analyticity, given that there's no principled distinction between sentences we can become justified in believing through semantic competence alone (*analytic* sentences) and those we cannot (*syntactic* sentences). Whatever our epistemology of logic looks like, then, it cannot depend upon either intuition or analyticity.

This brings us to Quine's positive case for his own evidential holism, comprising two factors. First, his commitment to the Duhem-Quine thesis: that an individual hypothesis cannot be conclusively falsified (or verified) in isolation. Given that auxiliary hypotheses are required to deduce the testable consequences of a target hypothesis, when faced with recalcitrant data, we always have the choice of laying the blame on auxiliary hypotheses rather than the target hypothesis itself. Thus, which hypothesis should be rejected in such situations is underdetermined. Based upon this, Quine concludes that it is whole theories (including our accepted logic), and not individual hypotheses, that are (dis)confirmed by evidence. Once we accept that we do not have unmediated access to the correct logical laws, given that such laws cannot be tested in isolation, they must be justified as part of our overall 'web of belief'.

A consequence of the Duhem-Quine thesis is that it is always possible to rescue a particular belief or proposition within the overall web or theory in the face of recalcitrant data by making suitable alterations elsewhere in the system (Quine 1951: 38). The laws of logic are no different. Once one admits these laws into one's testable web, there is no principled reason to preclude them from being revised in the face of troublesome data. Granted, revisions to the logical laws should be a last resort, given their centrality in our web of belief and thus the extensive repercussions such a revision could have for our overall commitments (Quine 1950: xiv).[14] However, there is still no guarantee that rejecting the disjunctive syllogism or the law of excluded middle, say, won't be our best option in the face of extensive and drastic counterevidence:

> Logic is in principle no less open to revision than quantum mechanics or the theory of relativity ... If revisions are seldom proposed that cut so deep as to touch logic, there is a clear enough reason for that: the principle of minimum mutilation. The maxim suffices to explain the air of necessity that attaches to logical and mathematical truth (Quine 1986: 100).

This *maxim*, being the theoretical virtue of making as little change as needed to our current belief system in order to accommodate the recalcitrant data, so as not to simultaneously lose existent benefits of the system.

This brings us to Quine's second positive motivation for his evidential holism, his commitment to *empiricism*, intimately bound with his naturalism: '[I]t is a finding of natural science itself, however fallible, that our information about the world comes only through impacts on our sensory receptors' (1990: 19). Thus, to justify *any* claim, whether about the physical world, mathematics, or *logic*, we must look exclusively to those sources of evidence deemed

---

[14] Centrality being the suitable analogue of the presumed *generality* of logic within Quine's metaphor of the web.

naturalistically acceptable. There is no substantial divide between the evidence that motivates our choice of logic and justifies scientific theories.

Revisions to our logical theory, then, do not rest upon arguments from analytic truth or *a priori* sources, but upon the same considerations that motivate other revisions within our web of belief. Any justification (or revision) of our logic is performed as part of the evaluation of our overall web of belief, with the pertinent evidence not differing in kind from that used in assessing scientific theories.[15]

Importantly, Quine's proposal is justified *not* via detailed consideration of how logicians support their theories, but rather through three philosophical factors. First, a dissatisfaction with existent foundationalist epistemologies of logic. Assuming scepticism regarding logic is unsatisfactory, the failure of these foundationalist proposals entails the need for a novel non-foundationalist epistemology of logic: *evidential holism*, supported by a commitment to (i) the Duhem-Quine thesis and (ii) naturalism. Quine's justification for his epistemology of logic is, therefore, well and truly top-down. Unfortunately, the resulting proposal is at odds with logical research in several regards, each of which problematises the way logicians actually go about justifying logics.

First, Quine's holism requires us to see *all* scientifically respectable data as a possible motivation for revising our logic. In principle, at least, all such sources of data are treated the same in terms of their possible importance for logic. There should be no distinction between data pertinent to logic and data pertinent to other fields. Yet, this downplays the importance that certain types of evidence play within logic. For instance, the logico-semantic paradoxes are not simply one form of recalcitrant data to be treated alongside results from the natural sciences. No prominent research programme in logic is (re-)assessed on the basis of its ability to make sense of findings from the biological sciences. Instead, the majority of contemporary arguments for non-classical logics are based upon their ability to solve open puzzles highlighted by the logico-semantic paradoxes, which classical logic (putatively) cannot; paracomplete logics are justified on the basis of the semantic paradoxes regarding truth (Field 2008), paraconsistent logics on the basis of set-theoretic paradoxes (Priest 2006b), and supervaluationist logic on the basis of the sorites (Fine 1975). Thus, while it's true, as we'll see in the following sections, that certain theoretical commitments from mathematics and linguistics are deemed relevant to the logical enterprise, our best theories of astrophysics and

---

[15] It is this proposed epistemic continuity between logic and the sciences that has led some to cite Quine as the paradigm anti-exceptionalist about logic (Wright 2021). More on this in the following sections.

microbiology are not.[16] Yet, in virtue of logicians not actively allowing findings from these fields to inform our logic, Quine's evidential holism deems the current practice of logicians wholly *inappropriate*.

Second, due to the *maxim of minimum mutilation*, Quine's holism proposes that we should only expect revisions to logic to be entertained in the most drastic of situations, when all other attempts to 'save the data' have failed. This is a result of our logical commitments having a privileged position at the centre of the web of belief, and thus any alterations to these commitments potentially having far-reaching repercussions. Yet, as shown by those non-classical logics devised in the face of logico-semantic paradoxes, revising one's logic is not seen merely as the final drastic option when all other avenues are closed off. Rather, it's a viable option to take even when other routes are available. We know this because there are classical solutions on the table for each paradox, which allow us to accommodate the recalcitrant data by making alterations elsewhere in the web. Thus, while it may always be *possible* to save the data without revising one's logic, these are not the only reasonable options entertained by contemporary logicians.

As far as Quine's holism is concerned, contemporary non-classical logicians are doing something methodologically *inappropriate* by attempting to replace the successfully established logic when other revisions are available. Yet, it is one matter to claim that non-classical logicians are *mistaken* in their revisionary arguments, and another to assert that they are acting methodologically *inappropriately*. Rarely do classically minded logicians respond to their non-classical colleagues by accusing them of inappropriate methods simply in virtue of non-classical solutions being touted while classical solutions are available. Rather, it's recognised that the overall benefits of the competing solutions must be assessed. Again, Quine's holism unnecessarily problematises an important feature of how logicians justify their theories.

2.4 Reasons for Optimism

Here we have a clear case in which a top-down approach to logic's epistemology delivers an over-idealised account that problematises how logicians justify their theories. Fortunately, there is reason for optimism, for we have seen how similar problems posed by top-down approaches within the philosophies of science and mathematics have been resolved by embracing a practice-oriented approach. There is good reason to think, then, that in principle the same can be

---

[16] Indeed, the often-cited example of empirical evidence being used to support a logic, Putnam's (1969) argument for quantum logic in the face of the measurement problem, is a complete outlier. It is notable that the proposal never truly gained traction.

achieved for the epistemology of logic. By basing our account of logic's epistemology upon the means through which logicians actually justify their theories, we can expect to rectify those concerns raised against Quine's proposal. It is one thing to be optimistic, however, and another to deliver on these promises. Demonstrating the practice-based approach *can* deliver is our goal in the final section. Before we get there however, we must first consider our final shortcoming to avoid: assuming that logic's epistemology is inherently different from that of other areas, especially the recognised sciences.

3 Foundationalism and the Exceptionality of Logic

So far, we have argued that to understand the epistemology of *logic*, we need to move beyond simply investigating the conditions for good (logical) reasoning and consider how we justify our endorsement of particular *logics*. Further, that the best means to gain this understanding is not based on conceptual analysis or standing assumptions about the nature of logic, but by looking at what logicians actually do, using a practice-based approach. This section addresses a third common perception regarding logic that can hinder our understanding of its epistemology: the idea that logic stands apart from the recognised sciences in terms of its epistemology.

Tradition has it that logic is exceptional (Martin and Hjortland 2022). Unlike the laws of other areas of inquiry, those of logic apply equally to all domains. To this extent, logic is not concerned with the particular identity of any object or property. Indeed, logic is not concerned with the content of propositions at all, but only with their formal structure. For this reason, logical laws are not responsive to the peculiarities of events in the actual world as those of the sciences are. Consequently, if they are known, its laws must be known in a wholly different fashion.

Our focus here is on those *epistemic* properties which putatively make logic special and differentiate it from the sciences; in particular, the *foundational* status of logical justification. While in the sciences and mathematics we often presume the validity of specific logical inferences to establish conclusions from some given data or axioms, respectively, within logic it appears we cannot do this without begging the question. Accordingly, justification for logic must be *non-inferential* and, thus, epistemically *self-supporting*.

We have two aims in this section. First, to highlight the motivations for thinking that logic's epistemology is distinct from that of the sciences, in virtue of being *foundational*. Second, to show that the two most prominent foundationalist pictures of logic's epistemology, *logical rationalism* and *semanticism*, are inadequate because they are inconsistent with how logicians justify their logics. This subsequently motivates our discussion of non-foundationalist epistemologies of logic in the next section, and our resulting claim that the mechanisms of theory-choice in logic are not that different from those in the sciences.

3.1 The Foundational Status of Logic

In general, to say that a belief is *epistemically foundational* just means, firstly, that our justification for that belief is *self-sustaining* and so does not depend for its justification on any other belief, and secondly, that our justification for some other beliefs depends (at least partially) on our having justification for these foundational beliefs. Thus, to say that (some of) our beliefs regarding logic are epistemically foundational means that our justification for these beliefs is *self-sustaining* and that they serve to (partially) justify other beliefs we possess.[17]

Historically, there have been two reasons to be tempted to endorse foundationalism about logic. Firstly, it allows one to address sceptical concerns not only over the logical laws themselves but also over other putative items of knowledge that evidentially depend upon logic, such as those of mathematics. If each of our beliefs requires justification, then to avoid an infinite regress, some of these beliefs must have self-sustaining justifications, and those regarding logic are the most suitable candidates. This justification for logical foundationalism is most apparent with the logicists, such as Frege, who seek to ground (or explain) mathematical facts in terms of logical facts. While we're told that many arithmetical truths lack self-evidence and thus require proof, the primitive logical laws are themselves self-evident and so require no further argument (Frege 2013 [1893]: vi–xvii). Thus, these primitive logical laws can (purportedly) bear the foundational weight of mathematics.

Secondly, foundationalism is a natural response to concerns over the inevitable bootstrapping that occurs if we use non-logical beliefs to justify logical laws. Any epistemology of logic which proposes that we become justified in believing a logical law L in virtue of appealing to other commitments C will face problems, the foundationalist says, for we will always need to appeal to *logical rules* to demonstrate that C are (in)consistent with L. In other words, any non-foundationalist justificatory process for logical laws requires making *deductive inferences*.

However, of course, any logical rules relied upon in making such inferences will either need to be sanctioned by the set of logical laws under consideration

---

[17] Remember, we're concerned here with our justification for beliefs *about* logic, constituting our warrant for endorsing particular logics, not our justification for *making inferences* deemed logical. This raises the question of what exactly the subject matter(s) of these beliefs are: rules of inference, argument schema, whole logics, or something else? This will be an ongoing concern for this section and the next. For the moment, we'll speak generically of logical *laws*.

or not. If they are, then the advocate of the laws is simply begging the question by relying upon the rule for the laws' evidential support. In contrast, if the laws *fail* to sanction the deduction's validity, then, assuming there's no alternative *non*-logical justification for the deduction, the laws undercut their own justification; the deduction turns out not to be justified after all. Either way, justification for *at least some* logical laws must be non-inferential.

This concern over non-foundationalist epistemologies of logic, known as the *centrality problem* (Wright 1985) or *background logic problem* (Martin 2021b; Woods 2019), is the main motivation for contemporary foundationalist epistemologies of logic (BonJour 1998). It has similarity to those traditional concerns raised against circular arguments motivating foundationalist responses to the infamous Pyrrhonian challenge. But, in this instance, the troublesome cases are not explicitly *premise*-circular but rather *rule*-circular, in that any non-foundationalist argument for a logic presupposes the validity of a rule of inference in reasoning to the justificatory argument's conclusion, rather than explicitly including the concluding logical law as a premise.[18]

Once one admits that our justification for (a subset of) the logical laws is foundationalist, two further properties of logic likely follow: First, that there is some *identifiable conscious property* associated with this foundational justification. Given that foundationalism requires one to be justified in believing these logical laws without any evidential support from further beliefs, to have *conscious access* to the epistemic good standing of these laws, there must be some identifiable property of the relevant belief states associated with their self-sustaining status, such as *self-evidence*. Of course, this does not *require* that there is such an associated identifiable property, for it is a possibility that, while we have self-sustaining justification for particular logical laws, we can never recognise when we, in fact, do. Yet, this would be an unsatisfying result for any foundationalism regarding logic, given the need to answer the question of why we should endorse a set of logical laws L_1 rather than another, L_2.[19]

Second, in virtue of the justification being non-inferential, these logical laws must be justified by *a priori* sources. This is due to two factors. Firstly, the possibility of *inferring* evidence for these specific laws from empirical evidence is precluded by their foundational status; the evidence for these privileged laws is *non-inferential*. Secondly, while this does not preclude the possibility of non-inferential perceptual evidence supporting these foundational laws, there are no viable observable states of affairs that *directly* demonstrate that logical laws are true. We do not perceptually see that

---

[18] Thus, providing distinct justificatory mechanisms for the belief in the resulting logical law and the inferences that produced the justified belief in the law may solve the problem.
[19] Shapiro (2009) makes a similar point regarding foundationalism in mathematics.

modus tollens or contraposition is valid, for instance. Thus, if our justification for logical laws is self-sustaining, it is also *a priori*.

3.2 Foundationalist Epistemologies of Logic

Two proposals have dominated the foundationalist literature: logical *rationalism* and *semanticism*. While both agree that the justification for (some) logical laws must be non-inferential and *a priori*, they disagree on the source of this *a priori* evidence.

For rationalists, one becomes justified in believing logical laws via a *quasi-perceptual* intellectual faculty, commonly known as *intuition* or *mental insight*, in which one *non-perceptually sees* that a law is true (BonJour 1998). Such intuitions are now commonly understood as being phenomenologically similar to perceptual states and, therefore, able to represent states of affairs (Chudnoff 2011), providing us with evidence for the truth or falsity of their contents, including logical laws:

> When you have an intuition that A, it *seems* to you that A ... [understood as a] genuine kind of conscious episode. For example, when you first consider one of de Morgan's laws, often it neither seems true nor seems false; after a moment's reflection, however, something happens: it now just seems true. (Bealer 1998: 207)

Thus, we simply *non-perceptually* see that the relevant law is true. In this regard, our justification for logical laws is like that for other (putative) necessary truths, such as conceptual truths (Chudnoff 2011).

In contrast, *semanticists* deny the need to posit a novel cognitive faculty to accommodate logical justification. Instead, justification for logical laws is understood in terms of linguistic proficiency; in virtue of understanding the meaning of the constituent terms of a logical law, we automatically become justified in assenting to its truth:

> If one knows what is the function of the words 'either', 'or', and 'not', then one can see that any proposition of the form 'Either p is true or p is not true' is valid. (Ayer 1936: 79)[20]

That is, logical laws are *epistemically analytic*.

---

[20] Notice that the purported logical law here takes the form of a *quasi-natural language schema*, not one within a logic's object language. This should already raise one's suspicions about whether semanticism can plausibly explain how we come to justify those laws constituting our fully-fledged logical theories, rather than simply believing that arguments of a certain quasi-natural language schema are 'good'. In other words, semanticism mistakes *Good Schema* justification for logical justification proper.

Which of these foundationalist pictures one endorses has tended to depend upon one's further philosophical commitments, including one's metaphysical views about logic and the viability of non-naturalistic sources of evidence. In other words, based upon *top-down* considerations.

For instance, semanticists, such as the logical positivists, were motivated to accept logic's analyticity based upon their scepticism over the existence of a special cognitive faculty providing direct insight into the truths of logic and, further, the desire to accommodate the putative necessary truth of logical laws without having to rely on the dubious notion of metaphysical necessity (Carnap 1963: 46). By embracing the joint *metaphysical* and *epistemological* analyticity of logical laws, the semanticists hoped to simultaneously account for the apparent necessary truth of logic's laws in terms of linguistic conventions, rather than the ways the world must be, while explaining our justification for embracing these laws in virtue of appropriately grasping their semantic content (akin to other humdrum analytical truths, such as 'All female foxes are vixens').

In comparison, rationalists desire to uphold the objectivity of logic, which they believe the semanticist has thrown away by demoting logic to the status of conventions (BonJour 1998). This they often attempt to achieve by rejecting naturalism and admitting both abstract non-spatiotemporal facts and a special faculty *rational intuition* to access them (Katz 1998).

Thus, neither rationalists nor semanticists are generally motivated by the forms of evidence logicians actually appeal to when justifying their logics. Rather, beginning with the standing assumption that our justification for (some) logical laws must be non-inferential and *a priori*, it's presumed that a position such as rationalism or semanticism must be correct if we're to avoid the unfortunate sceptical conclusion that we fail to possess knowledge about logic (Boghossian 2000). Further, the answer to which of these candidates one should favour is made not on the basis of which provides us with a more realistic answer to logical justification but, firstly, which is more suitable to avoid unwanted sceptical conclusions and, secondly, which is compatible with further commitments their advocates embrace, such as naturalism or realism about logical facts.

Given our case for the practice-based approach in the previous section, the pertinent question for us here is not whether either of these proposals delivers on their top-down goals. That is an ineffective means to determine the accuracy of an epistemology of logic. Rather, we are concerned with how plausible both proposals are, given what we know about how logics are assessed. In particular, the extent to which the positions problematise the actual debates logicians have over the correct logical laws and the forms of evidence they use. Whatever other virtues an epistemology of *logica artificialis* possesses, if it cannot make sense of a vast array of the ways in which logicians go about justifying their theories, this is a problem for the epistemological theory, not the practitioners.

3.3 Challenges to the Foundational Picture

To adequately assess these foundationalist epistemologies in light of logical practice, we must first understand what we would *expect* logic's epistemology to look like if either proposal were true.

According to rationalism, we gain justification for (foundational) logical laws directly from intuitions regarding the law. We simply *see* that it's true. Thus, if rationalism were true, we would expect arguments over the correct logic to be full of appeals to intuitions, especially when it comes to those fundamental laws on which the remainder of one's logic rests. Similarly, when there is disagreement over the truth of important claims, we ought to find the parties straightforwardly appealing to their intuitions regarding the truth of the relevant claims. Indeed, for the rationalist, there is nothing else the logician *can* appeal to. If another party disagrees with us, all we can do is suggest that our interlocutor is not having the right kinds of intuitions and 'looks' a bit harder.

The semanticist is in a similar position. According to her, we gain justification for our logical laws directly by grasping their meaning. Once we understand their constituent parts, we become immediately justified in believing their truth. Thus, if there were any disagreement over a law's truth, one would expect to find each side appealing to the meaning of the relevant law to substantiate their own claims about its truth or falsity. If one's interlocutor fails to assent to the same laws as we do, we are committed to saying this is simply because they have misunderstood its content somehow. All we can do in this case, in the hope of rescuing the situation, is point out the law's meaning even more explicitly.

Now that we have a better understanding of what we would expect logical debates to look like were either rationalism or semanticism true, a few words of warning. Firstly, proponents of neither position are clear on the exact subject matter of these foundational beliefs: whether they are *rules of inference, argument schemas*, or something else. This poses a complication when it comes to assessing them. For instance, were we to focus on how logicians go about justifying the validity of rules of inference or argument schemas, it is always possible the foundationalist will respond that our criticisms miss their mark, as they were never concerned with the justification of these particular commitments in the first place, but rather something else. This is an unavoidable problem unless the foundationalist is willing to specify the exact form these foundational beliefs take.

Second, the foundationalist is not committed to *every* logical law (however conceived) being foundational and thus non-inferentially justified. Rather, all that is required is that some *privileged subset* of the laws is foundationally justified, with those other laws comprising the logic being derivatively justified. This causes another complication, for unless the foundationalist specifies which laws serve as foundations, we can never be sure we have evidence against their proposal; they can always explain away the troublesome cases by proposing that the specific law under consideration isn't foundational, and thus the fact that it isn't treated as such by logicians poses no problem for their account.

Fortunately, both complications have a reasonable solution. While there is more to a logic than the argument schema or rules of inference it validates, an important part of what constitutes disagreements between logics and the logicians who advocate them is the divergence over the respective sets of valid schema or rules of inference. Further, if foundationalism were true, then even if the putative (in)validity of these argument schema or rules of inference did not constitute the foundational logical beliefs for which we have non-inferential justification, we would expect disagreements over the argument schema or rules to eventually 'ground out' in a disagreement over one of the foundational logical commitments. After all, this is just the point of foundationalism: the foundational beliefs support non-foundational ones. Thus, if there is disagreement over whether a non-foundational rule of inference or argument schema is (in)valid, that disagreement must ultimately be caused by either a disagreement over the foundational beliefs justifying it or the reasoning from the foundational to non-foundational beliefs. Therefore, we can safely proceed and consider the ways in which logicians go about justifying their logics, containing sets of valid argument schema and rules of inference, in the knowledge that if these logics were ultimately justified on the basis of foundational logical commitments, this would exhibit itself in the form of appeals to intuitions regarding these commitments or definitions when disagreements arose.

Another complication, not so easily resolved, is the potential for the foundationalist to reject the association between a law's foundational status and its possession of some identifiable property, such as *self-evidence*. Doing so would, in effect, divorce the conscious justificatory processes exemplified by logicians' practice when engaged in theory choice from the reality of why we are *actually justified* in holding certain logical commitments. It would automatically ensure that nothing found within actual logical debates could contradict the foundationalist proposal, for we shouldn't expect foundationalism to have any *identifiable consequences* when it comes to the reasons logicians have access to and use in arguing for a logic.

When faced with this response, the best we can do is proceed regardless, in recognition that the less relationship foundationalism has to the reasons we have access to, the less relevant it is to those of us wishing to understand why humans are justified in endorsing one logic rather than another. Perhaps the reasons logicians give in support of their preferred logics are epiphenomenal, but in that case, it's unclear why we shouldn't say the same for scientists and mathematicians too. It is always possible to hypothesise a justificatory mechanism and suggest that, in reality, contrary to the appearances of what researchers in the field are doing, it is in fact this other (*non-apparent*) mechanism which justifies the relevant theories. But, in this case, I see the proposal as no more assessable than the existence of an undetectable particle.

Let us proceed, then, on the assumption that if foundationalism were true, we would see its effects in how logicians argue for their logics. We focus here on two concerns that are especially troublesome for foundationalism about logic: first, that logicians make few (if any) appeals to the self-evidence of a logical law, relying instead upon judgements over specific arguments to support their theories; second, that the logico-semantic paradoxes play an important role in the evaluation of logics.

3.3.1 Appeals to specific inferences, not logical laws

Firstly, if foundationalism about logic were true, we would expect disagreements over the correct logic to manifest themselves as straightforward appeals to competing laws. That, contrary to what's suggested by advocates of logic $\mathcal{L}_2$, some law or commitment L within $\mathcal{L}_1$ is self-evident. If advocates of $\mathcal{L}_2$ cannot appreciate this fact, that is their own shortcoming; they are either having mistaken intuitions regarding L or do not fully understand its content.

Yet rarely, if ever, do logicians directly appeal to the self-evidence of particular *laws* or theoretical commitments. In contrast, appeals are made to the acceptability of *specific* arguments or inferences. The (putative) acceptability of this specific inference is then used as data to criticise competing logics for their inability to sanction this inference with the laws they contain. Let's consider a few brief examples of this phenomenon.

First, take Williamson's (1994) examination of multi-valued solutions to the sorites. Rather than directly appealing to the correctness of the classically valid rules of inference which the non-classical logics invalidate, in order to undermine the latter logics, Williamson produces examples of *specific inferences* that we deem acceptable but which the non-classical logics deem invalid. For instance, Williamson (1994: 106) criticises Hallden's three-valued gappy logic for deeming the inference from 'Jack is not a philosopher' to 'Jack is not a *bald* philosopher' invalid when Jack is a *borderline case* of baldness, although the inference is perfectly fine regardless of Jack's relative state of baldness. Thus, the logic is criticised for its inability to sanction *specific inferences* we find acceptable.

Another example comes from Burgess's (1983) criticism of relevant logics for invalidating the disjunctive syllogism. Again, in substantiating his concern, Burgess does not simply appeal to the self-evidence of the disjunctive syllogism. Rather, he points out that informal mathematical proofs make prominent use of inferences (putatively) sanctioned by the rule. Burgess's argument differs from Williamson's only in that, instead of citing specific examples of informal proofs that (putatively) require the disjunctive syllogism to substantiate their validity, he takes it as given that there are inferences within informal proofs that instantiate the natural-language schema:

$$\frac{A \text{ or } B \quad\quad\quad}{\text{not } B} \quad \text{(D)}$$
$$\overline{\quad A \quad}$$

Further, in virtue of such inferences occurring regularly within the reliable epistemic practice of mathematics, they must be *good* inferences.[21]

A similar argument is used by Tennant (2004) to criticise dialetheism, the view that some contradictions are true, whose advocates embrace a glutty paraconsistent logic (such as **LP**).[22] Tennant criticises such logics not on the basis that they invalidate certain rules of inference which are *self-evidently* true, but on the basis that, to the best of our knowledge, we *need* these rules to justify important inferential moves within mathematical proofs. If the dialetheist thinks he is wrong, they should show us *how* these informal proofs can be regimented within their logic. Thus, when challenged, logicians rarely attempt to establish the truth of a logical law based upon its self-evidence.

The same can be said for those *rejecting* a law. This is most obviously seen in the case of *direct* challenges to established classically valid laws with concrete counterexamples, such as McGee's (1985) famous putative counterexample to *modus ponens* and Yalcin's (2012) putative counterexample to *modus tollens* with conditionals containing a probability operator. In neither case are intuitions

---

[21] Note, Burgess is *not* assuming that instances of (D) exemplify the classically-valid disjunctive syllogism: $\{A \vee B, \neg B\} \vDash A$. After all, the validity of this latter schema is exactly what is up for debate with the relevant logician. Rather, the challenge Burgess poses the relevantist is whether they can explain with their own logic why instances of (D) in mathematics are acceptable.

[22] The *Logic of Paradox* (**LP**) is a three-valued logic, that uses the strong-Kleene matrices for the Boolean connectives but treats the third truth-value as the designated truth-value *both* (true and false).

regarding the law itself used to undermine the law. Rather, disconfirming instances are sought.

The strongest evidence we have against foundationalism, however, is not merely the *absence of* appeals to self-evidence, but the evidence we have that theory-choice in logic works through an *inferential, constructive process*. It is anything but unmediated. While logical laws impact our conclusions regarding the validity of natural-language arguments, such laws are not themselves expressed in a natural language. Logics are formulated in an artificial language, connected to natural-language arguments through translation (or representation) rules (Aberdein and Read 2009).[23] If foundationalism were true, we would expect logicians to appeal to the self-evidence of these logical laws in the artificial language *and then* argue, on the basis of establishing these laws, that particular natural-language arguments are valid given some suitable translation rules. In other words, while we have direct insight into the truth of certain logical laws, we then *infer* the validity of specific arguments.

However, the opposite is what we find in logical debates. It is the acceptability of specific inferences that is used to substantiate claims about the correctness of laws, not the other way around. If anything is taken as given (or self-evident) within logical debates, it is the acceptability of *specific* arguments or inferences, not the laws themselves.[24] Indeed, not only are appeals made to 'obviously' acceptable natural-language arguments, but such appeals often have evidential force because there is general agreement between the parties involved over the (un)acceptability of the pertinent arguments. What the parties tend to disagree over, instead, is how these acceptable arguments should be *formalised* into logical laws. Disagreement hinges, then, not on the self-evidence of a specific logical law, but on *how* to sanction the validity of these specific arguments within a logic.

The relevantist debate over the validity of disjunctive syllogism demonstrates this nicely. Though Anderson and Belnap (1975) reject the disjunctive syllogism, they agree with the classical logician that many arguments of the natural-language schematic form (*D*) are valid, particularly in mathematics. In other words, both parties agree over these instances but disagree over how the arguments should be formalised to explain their validity. This is demonstrated

---

[23] Talk of 'translation rules' does not imply there is a non-context dependent *mapping* between elements of the logic's object-language and parts of the natural language, any more than a translation between natural languages presumes a mapping between lexical items across the languages. We revisit this point in the following section.

[24] Note that this does not mean the *direction of explanation* is from the specific instances to the laws. As we'll see in the next section, it is perfectly consistent with this picture to suggest that the laws contained within a logic *explain why* particular natural-language arguments are valid. The question here is how we come to recognise the correct laws in the first place.

by relevant logicians taking on the burden of showing how the validity of these arguments can be accommodated with a new relevant surrogate of the disjunctive syllogism, using an intensional disjunction called *fission*. Thus, the classical logician wasn't mistaken about the natural-language arguments; they are indeed valid. They simply mistook them for instances of the classically-valid disjunctive syllogism. Instead, they are actually instances of the relevant logician's own version of the syllogism using an intensional disjunction. The focus of the disagreement then becomes whether either of these logical laws faithfully formalises the pertinent natural-language arguments (Lavers 1988).

A similar point can be made with the dialetheist's rejection of classical *modus ponens* using the material conditional.[25] They do so not based on finding the law self-evidently false, but because self-referential paradoxes (putatively) provide us with reason to believe that some propositions are *both* true *and* false (Priest 2006b); in other words, that *truth-value gluts* exist. If one keeps the standard semantics for disjunction and negation fixed, and understands logical consequence as truth-preservation, admitting truth-value gluts straightforwardly provides a countermodel to $\{A \rightarrow B, A\} \vDash B$; just allow A to be a glut while B is simply false.

Yet, in rejecting classical *modus ponens*, the dialetheist does not thereby claim that uses of a detachable conditional across mathematics and the sciences are generally invalid. They agree with the classical logician on the validity of vast swathes of arguments of the quasi-natural language form 'If A then B, A, therefore B' (and other expressions of the indicative conditional); they simply disagree over the logical law that explains the validity of these natural-language arguments. Again, this is shown by the dialetheist taking on the theoretical burden of finding a new conditional capable of sanctioning these *acceptable inferences* within the sciences while being compatible with their commitment to the existence of gluts.[26]

Even when there isn't agreement over the (un)acceptability of the specific inference, there is still a recognition that, because an inference's putative (un)acceptability is pertinent to evaluating a logic, any such evidence cannot be rejected out of hand but must be addressed somehow. This is shown by responses to McGee's counterexample to *modus ponens*. Rather than simply rejecting the troublesome case by appealing to the self-evidence of *modus ponens*, we instead find attempts to either: (i) explain away the putative counterexample by showing that it's not actually an instance of the law (Lowe 1987), or that it confuses *reasons to rationally believe* with *truth* (Sinnott-Armstrong et

---

[25] That is, the conditional $(A \rightarrow B)$ defined as $\neg A \vee B$.
[26] See Beall (2009) for the debate over the most suitable conditional for the dialetheist's purposes.

al. 1986), or (ii) accommodate it by providing a new unaffected version of *modus ponens* (Bledin 2015).

Exemplified by these cases is a mediated process in which our judgements over specific inferences *inform* our theory of logic, and we do our best to accommodate these judgements as data with our postulated laws. This, of course, requires *inferences* to be made from the specific arguments to the putative logical laws. All of which is contrary to what foundationalism proposes. The picture of logic's methodology we gain from these cases is *not* one of direct insight into logical laws, but a constructive process where laws are proposed to sanction arguments and inferences admitted as acceptable. Further, competing proposals are criticised on the basis of not successfully fulfilling these desiderata.

Before we move on to the challenge posed by the logico-semantic paradoxes, two further points about appeals to self-evidence within logic are noteworthy. First, while we have stressed the rarity of appeals to the self-evidence of logical laws, we do not claim they *never* occur. There are always outliers. However, in those rare cases where appeals *are made* to the self-evidence of laws, such appeals rarely gain any purchase, suggesting they are deemed evidentially empty by the community. For instance, one of the few instances where such an appeal is made, Slater's (1995) attempt to disprove dialetheism by claiming that, *by definition*, contradictories could never be jointly true, completely failed. Debate on the virtues (and vices) of dialetheism carried on regardless. This shows that logicians are generally not content to justify logics based upon appeals to the self-evidence of laws or definitions.

Second, when appeals to logical laws *are made*, they are not usually made within the context of providing new evidence for a logic. Rather, they are *post hoc* appeals, summarising aspects of our presently accepted logical theory, which has already been independently supported. In other words, they serve as reminders not to blindly revise that particular aspect of the theory, given that it has significant independent support. The appeals, then, do not themselves have any evidential weight. An example of this comes again from Williamson's (1994: §4.2) discussion of vagueness, where he criticises some non-classical semantics for failing to respect truth-functionality, which would lead to many of the advantages gained by classical logic being lost. In this role, such appeals to established laws seem hardly peculiar to logic; it is common within the sciences to appeal to a well-established law or theory as a *reductio* to some novel proposal. Yet, in this case, it is not the appeal to the law or theory itself which provides the *evidential* support, but the fact that it is already independently well-supported.[27]

---

[27] For more on the role of *post hoc* appeals in logical theory-choice, see Martin & Hjortland (2021).

3.3.2 Problems Accommodating the Role of Paradoxes

Foundationalism also has problems explaining the role of paradoxes within logic's epistemology. As we noted in the previous section, the logico-semantic paradoxes play a significant role within logical theory-choice; the Russell paradox has motivated paraconsistent logics (Priest 2006b), the Curry paradox substructural logics (Zardini 2011), and the sorites supervaluationist logic (Fine 1975).

Consider, for example, probably the most famous paradox of them all – the liar.[28] As has been known since Tarski (1944: 348–9), troublesome liar-like sentences can arise in any language that is *semantically closed*. That is, a language L in which: (i) any sentence s in L can be named by a term t belonging to L, and (ii) L's own semantics can be expressed within the language (e.g., that sentence s is true).

Further, when combined with the intuitively plausible unrestricted T-schema,

$$T(\ulcorner A \urcorner) \equiv A$$

and some rather uncontroversial rules of implication, it can be shown that any semantically closed language is *inconsistent*. Take, for instance, the *strengthened liar*:

$$(\lambda) \ulcorner \lambda \urcorner \text{ is not true}$$

Once we admit (λ) into our language with the unrestricted T-schema, it's straightforward to show by classically valid rules that a contradiction follows:

$\lambda \equiv \neg T(\ulcorner \lambda \urcorner)$ (L1–Strengthened Liar)
$T(\ulcorner \lambda \urcorner) \equiv \lambda$ (L2–Instance of T-Schema)
$T(\ulcorner \lambda \urcorner) \equiv \neg T(\ulcorner \lambda \urcorner)$ (L3–From L1-L2 by transitivity)
$T(\ulcorner \lambda \urcorner) \vee \neg T(\ulcorner \lambda \urcorner)$ (L4–Instance of LEM)
$T(\ulcorner \lambda \urcorner) \wedge \neg T(\ulcorner \lambda \urcorner)$ (L5–From L3-L4 by cases and adjunction)

Now, one might think it's bad enough to be able to show that any semantically closed language is inconsistent. However, the situation may actually be worse than this, if we determine that some of the (natural or formal) languages we use *are* semantically closed. In this case, the liar paradox would show not only that semantically closed languages are inconsistent, but that some contradictions really are true.[29] Obviously, this situation is intolerable for most. Specifically,

---

[28] The same points here could be equally well-made using other logico-semantic paradoxes. See Martin (2021b) and Martin & Hjortland (2021) for similar analyses of the Russell and Curry paradoxes, respectively. We restrict ourselves to the liar for brevity.

[29] For the case that our natural languages are semantically closed, see Priest (2006b).

it's incompatible with classical logic on the assumption that trivialism is false, given that everything follows from a contradiction in the logic.

The logician who wishes to avoid the drastic conclusion of true contradictions has three options. First, deny that any of our non-trivial languages are semantically closed, or act so as to restrict them. Doing so would block the possibility of liar sentences occurring within the languages in the first place. This is the option Tarski (1944) takes, proposing that any putative semantically closed language L be split into a hierarchy of languages, such that for any language L_n, no term within L_n could apply a semantic property to sentences in L_n itself. Thus, in terms of truth, this ensures that L_n could not express that sentences within its own language were true. Instead, to express the semantic properties of sentences within L_n, a metalanguage L_{n+1} is needed. To ensure the semantic properties of every language could be expressed, this hierarchy would then have to continue *ad infinitum*. Second, one could deny the unrestricted T-schema, for instance by suggesting the schema only applies to *grounded sentences*, such as those sentences A that satisfy $T(\ulcorner A \urcorner) \vee T(\ulcorner \neg A \urcorner)$ (Kripke 1975). Finally, one could reject the validity of a rule of implication or law used within the derivation of the contradiction. Paracomplete solutions, for instance, reject the law of excluded middle used in L4 (Field 2008), and non-transitive solutions reject the inference to L3 (Weir 2015). All solutions of this third kind require a move away from classical logic and advocacy of a competing logic.

Common to all solutions is the recognition that the paradox cannot be simply ignored. Ultimately, any alethic logic, classical or not, must get to grips with the logico-semantic paradoxes and show it can avoid their unsavoury consequences.[30] This prominent role paradoxes play within the motivation of logics raises a challenge for the foundationalist. After all, the solution to these paradoxes is not itself *immediate*. There are multiple options on the table, and their relative strengths must be assessed. Whether, for instance, we are best off rejecting semantic closure, the unrestricted T-schema, or a logical law (and, in this case, *which* law).

Yet, according to foundationalism, we have unmediated justification for the privileged logical laws. This means there should be no evidence or data from which one *draws inferential support* in favour of either the truth or falsity of these laws. The paradoxes are, of course, just such a piece of evidence from which logicians draw inferences in favour of one logic or another. Thus,

---

[30] The Russell paradox, and other associated set-theoretic paradoxes, may be an exception here. Most logicians are now happy to assume mathematicians found their own fix for the paradox, by replacing the Axiom of Comprehension with the Axiom of Specification in ZFC. Some dialetheists (Priest 2006b) tend to be the exception.

contrary to what logical practice suggests, paradoxes can play no evidential role within logic for foundationalist epistemologies.

How can the foundationalist address this worry? After all, it's beyond doubt that paradoxes play an important role within the assessment of logics. First, they could claim that those laws impacted by the paradoxes are only non-privileged, non-foundational laws. However, given that just the liar paradox on its own raises the possibility of rejecting the law of excluded middle, *modus ponens*, and transitivity, this seems unlikely. For this reply not to be empty, the foundationalist would need to supply us with some indication of what these foundational laws are.

Second, they could restrict the role that paradoxes play within logic. Rather than providing evidence for or against the foundational laws for which we have self-sustaining justification, paradoxes merely serve to deliver *error messages* that something has gone awry. In other words, while paradoxes cannot constitute evidence for or against a *logic*, they can serve as an indicator of the unreliability of our intuitions or semantic judgements in a particular case. Thus, paradoxes would be limited to the role of *undermining*, rather than *overriding*, defeaters.

However, this solution seems unviable. First, it's unclear *why* paradoxes would be capable of demonstrating that our logical intuitions or semantic judgements are unreliable. Giving paradoxes this role suggests our justification for logical laws answers to something other than rational insight (or semantic judgements), and, again, this is explicitly rejected by foundationalist proposals; when it comes to the privileged foundational laws, at least. This concern emphasises the wider point that an adequate epistemology of logic should not only be able to detail *how* paradoxes factor into the evaluation of logics, but *why* they are capable of doing so.

Second, this concessionary role for the paradoxes is far from the substantive role they actually play within theory choice. Paradoxes serve not just to highlight the unreliability of our intuitions or linguistic judgements but also provide evidence *for* or *against* a logic in virtue of its (in)ability to effectively solve them. Foundationalist epistemologies of logic, thus, are ill-suited to make sense of the role paradoxes play within logic's epistemology.

This section has shown there is strong evidence against epistemological foundationalism with regard to logical laws. However, these insights from logical practice provide not only evidence against foundationalism but also prima facie support for a non-foundationalist epistemology of logic. After all, as we have seen, it is common for logicians to argue for a logic based on its ability to accommodate relevant data in the form of *specific inferences* generally deemed *(un)acceptable*. With this in mind, the next section assesses the prospects for a non-foundationalist epistemology of logic that can make sense of the reasons logicians provide in support of their theories. It turns out there is such an account, *logical predictivism*, which proposes that the mechanisms of theory-choice in logic are far more similar to those of the sciences than traditionally thought.

4 An Epistemology of *Logica Artificialis*

As we saw in the previous section, contrary to what's been traditionally proposed, there are good reasons to think logicians do not have direct access to the correct logical laws. This provides some initial motivation, at least, to consider the viability of a *non*-foundationalist epistemology of logic. Non-foundationalist epistemologies of logic differ from foundationalist proposals by recognising that logicians do not have *unmediated access* to the correct logical laws. Rather, to discover these laws, inferences must be made from some relevant data to inform and test theories. Any non-foundationalist proposal, therefore, must offer an account of what constitutes these relevant data while specifying the mechanisms by which logics are assessed against them. In what follows, we present a particular non-foundationalist epistemology of logic, *logical predictivism*, which argues, based upon logical practice, that logics are justified and ultimately chosen on the basis of their predictive success, explanatory power, and compatibility with other well-evidenced commitments, just as scientific theories often are.

Predictivism is an interesting proposal not only for its ability to specify the mechanisms and data by which logics are assessed, but it also shows how an informative epistemology of logic can be built upon logicians' practice, providing additional support for a practice-based approach to logic's epistemology. Further, by highlighting similarities between the methods of theory-choice in logic and the sciences, predictivism calls into question our traditional assumption that logic's epistemology is significantly different from these research areas.

Predictivism is by no means the only non-foundationalist epistemology of logic on the market. We have already considered an alternative, Quine's evidential holism, and seen some of its weaknesses. Other proposals include *reflective equilibrium* (Peregrin and Svoboda 2017) and *abductivism* (Priest 2016; Russell 2019; Williamson 2017). Ideally, we would have considered the strengths and weaknesses of each individually. However, doing so is beyond the scope of this section.[31] Instead, we begin our discussion with a rudimentary

---

[31] For critical discussion of reflective equilibrium and abductivism, see Martin (2024) and Martin and Hjortland (2021), respectively.

version of non-foundationalism about logic, naïve inductivism. This will be instructive, as it highlights problems non-foundationalist accounts can easily fall into but which predictivism avoids, allowing us to appreciate its strengths.[32]

4.1 Naïve Inductivism about Logic

We begin with the working assumption that the primary data logicians use to inform their theories are *judgements* about specific arguments or inferences, not empirical observations or something else. This is justified primarily by our findings from the previous section; logicians appeal to the acceptability of specific inferences to justify logical laws, not to the laws' self-evidence directly.[33] The question, then, is how exactly these judgements over specific inferences inform logics.

The most straightforward answer, which we'll call *naïve inductivism*, is that the laws constituting the logic are mere *extrapolated generalisations* from these instances. A view reminiscent of this is suggested by Bolzano (1972 [1837]: §315.4) in his account of how the syllogistic forms were established:

> The only reason why we are so certain that the rules *Barbara, Celarent*, etc., are valid is because they have been confirmed in thousands of arguments in which we have applied them.

Thus, laws regarding valid forms are the result of straightforward extrapolations from instances of natural-language arguments we deem valid. For instance, one notes that both of the following *seem* valid:

---

[32] Not all epistemologies of logic fit neatly into either of the foundationalist or non-foundationalist camps. Take, for instance, the *entitlement view*, that one is entitled in believing a logical law if it's *impossible to doubt it* (Wright 2004); with entitlement being the possession of epistemic warrant *without* cognitive access to the reasons for this warrant. According to this view, given that to call into question the truth of certain logical laws, such as *modus ponens* and universal instantiation, one ends up having to *use* instances of these very laws, this question begging undercuts any potential sceptical doubts over their truth. Further, once one appreciates one's entitlement to these fundamental laws, one can then use this entitlement to both *infer* other non-fundamental logical laws and construct a rule-circular proof of the fundamental laws themselves, allowing us to gain cognitive access to our reasons for endorsing the laws and thus full-blown *justification* for them. Therefore, unlike with foundationalism, we do not have direct cognitive access to our justification for, and so to the truth of, the privileged logical laws. Instead, we must construct rule-circular proofs of them. However, unlike non-foundationalist proposals, certain logical laws do have epistemic good standing prior to our providing evidence for them via data. While we're sceptical that the entitlement view can provide an account of our justification for *logics*, rather than simply what we've called *Good Schema* justification (see Martin 2024 for an analogous concern with reflective equilibrium), a full consideration of the proposal is beyond this section's scope.

[33] Of course, this does not tell us yet *whose* judgements ought to be used as a reliable guide to the truth of a logic, nor what justifies logicians' presumption that these judgements are a *reliable guide*. More on this below.

The train to Florence is going to be late, and I'll miss the flight if it's late, so I'm going to miss my flight.

It's going to be wild tonight. Tom's going to be at the party, and whenever Tom's there, things get wild.

Then, based on these arguments, one extrapolates to the generalisation they are putatively instances of. In this case, in all likelihood, *modus ponens*.[34]

One then seeks confirmation (or falsification) of these putative laws by finding further instances of the generalisations. If enough relevant instances are deemed valid, the law is confirmed. Conversely, if a sufficient number are found to be invalid, it's falsified.

Two features of this proposal make the inductivism *naïve*. First, the resulting theory is nothing but the union of these generalisations resulting from the extrapolations. Thus, some logic $\mathcal{L}$ is constituted *wholly* of a set of law-like generalisations $L_1, \ldots, L_n$, each of which has an associated supporting data set $D_1, \ldots, D_n$ comprising natural-language instances of the respective law-like generalisation.

Second, the data informing the generalisations has the *same content* as the resulting laws. After all, the laws are a result of *mere extrapolations* from the instances. Thus, those judgements constituting the data are about the *validity* of the specific natural-language arguments, just like the laws are about the validity of (forms of) arguments. This means that for the theory to be tested, no indirect consequences of the laws need to be inferred, nor operationalisation of the laws required; one simply searches for (dis)conforming instances.

There are undoubtedly attractive features of the inductivist picture. First, it does not require us to have unmediated access to the correct logical laws. Rather, it simply presupposes that some agents are reliable at recognising when some specific inferences are (in)valid, allowing us to avoid concerns raised against foundationalism. Further it offers a straightforward picture of how logicians arrive at their logics based upon these specific judgements: the laws are simply extrapolated generalisations from these (valid) argument instances.

Despite this, with its simplicity and *naïveté* come weaknesses. Many of these are recognisable from those that befall naïve inductivism in the sciences, with its oversimplified picture of theory-choice.

First, there are those problems resulting from the suggestion that the laws are a result of *direct extrapolation* from instances of these law-like generalisations

---

[34] What form does *modus ponens* (and the other laws) take in this scenario? Is it expressed in some schematized quasi-natural language, such as 'If X then Y, X, therefore Y', or the logic's object language (e.g., $\{\varphi \to \psi, \varphi\} \vDash \psi$)? We come to this below.

The Epistemology of Logic 49

with the *same content*. This is inconsistent with the content of logical laws and their relationship to natural-language instances in three respects.

One, logical laws are generalisations about *argument forms* in some sense. Thus, to suggest we can arrive at these logical laws by direct extrapolation from concrete arguments or inferences implies that the logical form of any given argument or inference is *transparent* to us. But this is clearly not the case. If it were, Frege's proposal to understand the form of arguments in terms of the function-argument distinction, rather than the long-standing subject-predicate distinction, would not have been so revolutionary. Further, we would not have those disagreements between logicians over the correct logical form of specific arguments that we do. For instance, there would be no disagreement between the classical and relevant logicians over whether arguments such as:

> Either there are Siegel zeros or there are infinitely many twin primes. There are no Siegel zeros, so there are infinitely many twin primes,

should be parsed as instances of the classically-valid $\{\varphi \vee \psi, \neg\varphi\} \vDash \psi$ with an extensional disjunction, or the relevantly-valid $\{\varphi + \psi, \neg\varphi\} \vDash \psi$ with an intensional disjunction.

Given that the logical forms of specific arguments are not transparent to us, our conclusion that an argument form is (in)valid – that is, whether a particular logical law is true or not – cannot be made on the basis of a mere extrapolation from argument instances. More complicated methodological work, including hypothesising the logical form of argument instances and associating these data with specific logical laws, must be at play. Concluding that an argument form is valid is not akin to concluding that 'All swans are white' on the basis of observing a thousand white swans. Call this the *transparency problem*.

Second, if logical laws were mere extrapolations from argument instances, we would expect these laws to take the form of implicit generalisations of schematised quasi-natural language arguments, such as:

> All arguments of the form 'If X then Y, X, therefore Y' are valid.

Yet, our laws do not take this form. They are expressed in the object-language of our theory. For instance, within classical logic, *modus ponens* takes the form $\{\varphi \rightarrow \psi, \varphi\} \vDash \psi$, with the conditional defined as $\neg\varphi \vee \psi$. Of course, given a suitable translation manual between the natural-language arguments and the logical laws, the laws have repercussions for whether arguments in the natural language are valid or not; but they are not themselves expressed in the natural language.

To suggest that logical laws are quasi-natural language generalisations would be to neglect the theoretical work that goes into providing formal models of the validity of natural-language arguments, capable of *explaining* their validity rather than merely serving as schematic generalisations. We have already warned against assimilating generalisations over schematised quasi-natural language arguments and logical laws in prior sections. At present, naïve inductivism seems capable of only providing us with *Good Schema* justification. Logical laws are not generalisations expressed in our everyday language; they require theoretical posits, just as scientific theories do. Thus, for an evidential connection to be established between logical data and the theory, a translation manual between the two is required. Call this the *translation problem.*

Third, pushing the problem one step further, we can ask whether it's even reasonable to think of our logical data and theories as having the same content, regardless of language. It is common within the sciences to distinguish the content of *data*, deemed a reliable indicator of some phenomenon, from the content of the theory itself, which is actually *about* the target phenomenon. For instance, while the various equations for alpha and beta radiation decay in nuclear physics are *about* the phenomenon of radiation decay, we do not directly observe these particles or their decay. Rather, we study their decay (among other means) by observing their condensation trails in a cloud chamber. Thus, there's an important data-phenomenon distinction to be respected (Bogen and Woodward 1988); rarely do our data take the form of direct observation (or detection) of the target phenomenon. Instead, appealing to auxiliary assumptions, we operationalise the consequences of our theory to test them against detectable data.

In contrast, by requiring our logical laws to be mere extrapolations from data instances, naïve inductivism dictates that the data must have the same content as the laws, collapsing the data-phenomenon distinction. This poses an obvious problem for logic, for our theories contain laws about which argument forms are *valid*, not simply those we find acceptable. Thus, for our attitudes towards the natural-language instances to have the same content as the laws, our judgements about these instances must be that they are *(in)valid*. Yet, there's good reason to deny that the content of these judgements we have about arguments is regarding their *logical (in)validity.*

First, the concept VALIDITY as used within contemporary logic is a technical concept understood (often) in terms of quantification over (sets of) models or the existence of proofs, subsequently used to *explain why* a given argument is good. Yet, it's implausible that even a very reliable reasoner, such as a mathematician who hasn't taken a discrete mathematics course, has the phenomenon of validity *in mind* when judging a step within an informal proof to be *good* or *acceptable*. To suggest such a thing is to neglect the innovative theoretical work that was required to get from our initial state of appreciating that an argument (or inference) is good, to understanding *why*, which included positing the technical concept of VALIDITY.

Second, logics are not concerned with all cases of deductive implication. There is an established distinction between *logical* implication – including some notion of validity *due to form* – and implications that are mathematical or lexical in nature. For instance, those inferences in graph theory whose validity relies upon the content of defined concepts such as (UN)DIRECTED GRAPH, VERTICES, and EDGES, or the lexical inference from 'We loaded the truck with hay' to 'We loaded hay on the truck' (Anderson 1971), neither of which is usually thought to be logical.

Yet, as we noted previously, there is no evidence that individuals are sensitive to the difference between logical and non-logical implications when judging whether a particular argument is good. Further, the question of where to draw this line between (non-)logical implications is an ongoing topic for philosophers (Sher 1991). Yet, if we suppose that the contents of reasoners' judgements are the same as the subject matter of our logical laws, much of this theorising would be unnecessary. We could make the distinction purely based on those inferences reasoners judged to be *logically* valid, or just mathematically/lexically acceptable.

Thus, we have good reason to think those judgements regarding specific arguments which inform our logic are not about the *logical (in)validity* of those arguments, but some other property. To test our logics against this data, a process of operationalisation is required, associating the subject matter of the theory (namely, *validity*) with the detectable data. Call this the *data-phenomenon collapse problem*.

While the previous problems were a result of the naïve relationship proposed between the content of the data and our theory, the following problems result from presuming that each putative law can only be accepted or rejected on the basis of finding direct instances of the law, which we judge to be (in)valid or (un)acceptable.

First, it's implausible that each law constituting our logic is individually justified through confirming instances. Not only are there too many laws, understood as valid argument forms, for us to 'check' individually against actual inferences, but there are multiple such forms deemed valid (for instance, by classical propositional logic) that either we don't have judgements regarding instances of, or it is difficult to even find instances of in our natural language due to their complexity. For instance, theorems containing embedded conditionals, such as Peirce's law and the conditional distribution laws (Martin and Hjortland 2021).

Given this, naïve inductivism has no plausible story for how these particular laws are supported, and thus why they are included within the accepted logic. Indeed, for any non-empty logic $\mathcal{L}_1$ constituted of the set of valid argument forms $\Gamma \cup \varphi$, there is another $\mathcal{L}_2$ constituted solely of Γ. Thus, without a story for how every such argument form φ can be directly supported by the available data, naïve inductivism is bound to have an incomplete picture of not only how the logical laws that constitute our preferred logic are justified, but why we should endorse our preferred logic $\mathcal{L}_1$ rather than $\mathcal{L}_2$. Call this the *incompleteness challenge*. This shows that an epistemology of logic must recognise that even if the validity of some argument forms can be directly evidenced by our judgements regarding instances, others must somehow be *derivatively evidenced*.

Inversely, naïve inductivism also has it that putative laws are *rejected* or *falsified* only on the basis of having direct contravening evidence against them, in the form of natural-language instances we deem invalid. However, logical laws are often rejected not because we have direct counterexamples against them, but because (combined with other laws) they entail a law that we *do* (putatively) have direct contravening evidence against. Thus, to not commit ourselves to some logical law L_1 for which we have direct contravening evidence, we must reject the union of some other laws $L_2, \ldots, L_n$.

This is exactly what we find in the relevant logician's rejection of the disjunctive syllogism. The law is rejected *not* because it has natural-language instances that are judged to be invalid. After all, the relevant logician admits we need a relevantly valid analogue to replace the seemingly reasonable, but ultimately mistaken, classical law to sanction acceptable inferences within informal proofs. Instead, the disjunctive syllogism is rejected because, in combination with the rule of addition and a suitable definition of validity, the law entails the validity of explosion, which (putatively) *does* have instances we judge to be unacceptable. What this shows is that our epistemology of logic must be able to explain not only our reasons to *accept* logical laws on the basis of derivative evidence but also our reasons to *reject* laws due to derivative evidence. Call this the problem of *bad company*.

Third, in suggesting that logical laws are *solely* justified by their putative instances, naïve inductivism ignores other prominent sources of evidence within logic. While our judgements over (putative) instances of a law do often constitute evidence for (or against) the law, such judgements are not exclusive as sources of evidence. As we saw, logics are also judged by their ability to solve certain open problems, such as the logico-semantic paradoxes. Yet, as far as naïve inductivism is concerned, given that the laws we settle on should be a direct result of those instances considered to be (in)valid, it is a mystery why logics should be assessed by their ability to solve these paradoxes. In this respect, naïve inductivism cannot make good sense of a significant portion of the reasons logicians give in support of their own, and against other, logics. Call this the problem of *mysterious sources*.

Finally, we have those problems associated with naïve inductivism's proposal that logical theories are wholly comprised of sets of laws, conceived as generalisations that arguments of a schematic form F are valid. However, logicians desire more from their theory than a set of generalisations which are extensionally adequate with regard to the set of valid arguments. They also wish for their theory to effectively *explain why* certain arguments are valid and others invalid.

This desire to provide an effective explanation of the (in)validity of arguments is most forcefully shown when logicians disagree over their theory of validity whilst agreeing over the *extension* of logical consequence. What occurs in these cases is extensionally identical logics with different semantics, favoured in virtue of their perceived explanatory power. For instance, while we have equally well-formulated, mathematically precise model-theoretic and proof-theoretic accounts of validity, each capable of delivering a classical consequence relation, logicians still find reasons to prefer one over the other on the grounds of *explanatory* superiority.

Advocates of the proof-theoretic account argue that it is explanatorily superior because it's able to specify the discrete steps needed to demonstrate that a given argument is valid, unlike the model-theoretic account (Prawitz 1985). Further, unlike the model-theoretic account, it doesn't require us to have a prior notion of (possible) 'models' to determine an argument's validity, which we must have to make sense of quantifying over all suitable models (Etchemendy 1990). In contrast, model-theoretic accounts have been deemed explanatorily more powerful, as they are able to specify the *exact* countermodels that show why a particular argument is invalid, as well as providing the counterfactual conditions under which alterations to an argument's logical form would make it valid or invalid (Martin 2021a).

This shows that logicians desire more from their logic than merely a set of generalisations identifying the valid argument forms; they also require it to effectively *explain* the validity of arguments. Given that straightforward generalisations over valid arguments don't constitute an explanation of *why* they are valid, but rather merely serve to sort valid from invalid arguments, naïve inductivism neglects the perceived explanatory value of logics, which has a noticeable impact on theory choice. Call this the problem of *extensional sufficiency*.

Thus, while naïve inductivism provides an attractively simple picture of how data, in the form of judgements over argument instances, could inform our logical theories, it suffers from multiple problems due to the way it conceives of this data, the relationship of the data to the theory, and the theory itself as comprised solely of schematic generalisations ranging over argument instances. Each of these weaknesses is informative when it comes to assessing predictivism.

4.2 Logical Predictivism[35]

Unlike naïve inductivism, predictivism does not propose that logics are the result of mere extrapolations from some data to the laws constituting the theory. Nor does it require that 'capturing' argument instances are the sole motivation of logicians when providing a theory of validity. There are various perceived 'open problems' that logicians are interested in solving, and the choice of which they focus upon can impact the logic they ultimately advocate. In this sense, it has similarities to the hypo-deductive picture of scientific inquiry, in which different motivating factors can lead to a hypothesis about the correct logic being initially proposed.

As with inductivism, however, predictivism recognises that logics are ultimately tested against data in the form of concrete arguments or inferences. While, given the perceived *generality* of logic, predictivism recognises that all manner of specific natural-language arguments are used to assess the adequacy of logics, for illustrative purposes, we use here examples of informal mathematical proofs. This is for good reason. First, these proofs played an important role within the development of classical logic, initially higher-order but then first-order, rectifying weaknesses with syllogistic logic. Second, as we've noted, even non-classical logicians who attempt to challenge classical logic tend to agree that the success of their theories partially depends upon their ability to successfully explain why these informal proofs are *good*. After all, mathematics is generally considered an important and successful intellectual enterprise concerned with what follows from what. Thus, these putative informal proofs are used as robust data against which to test candidate logics.[36]

---

[35] The presentation of predictivism here builds on Martin (2021a, 2024) and Martin & Hjortland (2021).

[36] This does not mean data from informal proofs will suffice in all cases of theory-choice. For instance, there are some phenomena which logics are interested in, such as counterfactuals, alethic modalities, and epistemic properties, which play a limited role in mathematical proofs. For this reason, evidence for logics dealing with these phenomena tend to focus on judgments regarding natural-language inferences, whether in scientific or everyday contexts (cf. Williamson 2007). We use data from informal proofs here as an exemplary and informative case. The *mechanisms* by which logics are tested against these natural-language arguments, according to predictivism, are in essence the same as for informal proofs; see Martin & Hjortland (2021) for details.

The question then is how these putative proofs, as a form of data, inform our logical theories. The logician begins with certain informal proofs, considered acceptable by mathematicians. For instance:

Theorem 1. *Assume $x \in \mathbb{Z}$. If $x^2 - 4x + 7$ is even, then x is odd.*

Proof. We prove our result indirectly. Suppose x is even, and let $x = 2k$ for some $k \in \mathbb{Z}$, so $x^2 - 4x + 7 = (2k)^2 - 4(2k) + 7$. Then, $(2k)^2 - 4(2k) + 7 = 4k^2 - 8k + 7 = 2(2k^2 - 4k + 3) - 1$, and so $x^2 - 4x + 7$ is odd. Thus, assuming x is even, $x^2 - 4x + 7$ is odd. □

Theorem 2. *For all $n \in \mathbb{Z}$. If $3n + 2$ is odd, then n is odd.*

Proof. We prove our result indirectly. Suppose n is even, and so $n = 2k$ for some $k \in \mathbb{Z}$. Consequently, $3n + 2 = 3(2k) + 2 = 6k + 2 = 2(3k + 1)$. But, then $3n + 2$ is even, as $2(3k + 1) = 2j$ for some $j \in \mathbb{Z}$, where $j = 3k + 1$. So, if n is even, then $3n + 2$ is even. □

Taking mathematicians' judgements over what constitutes a proof for a given theorem as a reliable (if fallible) guide as to which putative proofs actually are valid, the logician is then concerned with providing an explanation of *why* these two putative proofs are *good*, while others are not.

While our logician recognises that each proof contains its own specific features, including the manipulation of the equations in each, she also notices that there seems to be a general *form* they follow. Namely, that both claim to have proven that *if* some proposition φ holds, *then* another ψ also holds, on the basis that if ψ *fails* to obtain, φ also *fails* to obtain. In other words, that both contain the inferential step (S):

$$\frac{\text{If not } \psi \text{ then not } \varphi}{\text{If } \varphi \text{ then } \psi}$$

What we lack at present is any assurance that these two putative proofs, in fact, exhibit an inferential step of this 'schematic' form. Our logician may simply have interpreted them incorrectly. Predictivism does not make the mistake naïve inductivism does of assuming that the logical forms of arguments are somehow *transparent* to us. Every supposition regarding the form of a specific argument (or informal proof) requires hypothesising and judgement on the logician's part.

Further, even if these inferential steps within the two putative proofs did, in fact, instantiate this schematic form, there is no assurance that their instantiating it (partially) constitutes their being acceptable proofs. After all, our logician is aware that inferences can exhibit a whole host of different forms, many of which are irrelevant to their being good.

Finally, even if the logician becomes convinced that both putative proofs exemplify (*S*), and their exemplification of (*S*) partially constitutes their acceptability, this doesn't ensure that *all* putative proofs which exemplify this schematic form are good. At present, then, all we have is a hypothesis that the two putative proofs above exemplify the same basic form, that this schematic form is (*S*), and that their exemplifying this form partially constitutes their acceptability.

Our logician desires more than this, though. She wishes to understand the *general* rules that determine whether a putative proof is good or not, not simply what makes these two specific putative proofs good (if they are). Thus, based on this apparent similarity in (schematic) form of the two exemplar proofs, she puts forward a general hypothesis:

Hypothesis 1 All arguments of the form

$$\frac{\text{If not } \psi \text{ then not } \varphi}{\text{If } \varphi \text{ then } \psi}$$

are good.

Here we have the first explicit suggestion that inferences found across multiple proofs may be good *because* they share the same *underlying form*. This, of course, is the starting point for the enterprise of *formal* logic.

Yet, all we have so far is a generalisation, albeit one that can be falsified. We do *not* have an explanation of *why* arguments of this schematic form are good (if they are), and thus a (partial) explanation of why the putative proofs above are indeed proofs. Similarly, the generalisation 'All swans are white' does not explain *why* swans are white; for that, we require a genetic or evolutionary model.

Thus, to show *why* arguments of this schematic form are good (if they really are, that is), our logician needs an explanatory model. A theory which determines those characteristics of the arguments that allow us not only to differentiate 'good' argument forms from those which aren't, but also specifies *why* these forms are good (and others not). The postulates of such a theory would need to not only specify the various possible component parts of an argument, but also the properties of these constituent parts, how these constituent parts can be combined, and what it is for some propositions of a certain structure to *follow from* those of another structure. The theory would also need to include *representation* rules to translate between the data and theory.

It is here that we have our first attempt to explain *why* arguments are good in virtue of possessing a certain property, *validity*, determined by the underlying structures of these arguments. Here is a toy example of such a theory:

Theory A

Definition 1: Let $\neg \phi$ be Boolean negation.

Definition 2: Let $\phi \to \psi$ be Boolean material implication.

Formation Rule 1: If ϕ is a wff, then ⌜$\neg \phi$⌝ is a wff.

Formation Rule 2: If ϕ and ψ are wff, then ⌜$\phi \to \psi$⌝ is a wff.

Representation Rule 1: ⌜not ϕ⌝ = ⌜$\neg \phi$⌝.

Representation Rule 2: ⌜if ϕ then ψ⌝ = ⌜$\phi \to \psi$⌝.

Law 1: For every valuation, all propositions are either true or false, and not both.

Law 2: An argument is valid iff, for every valuation v, if every premise is true in v, the conclusion is true in v.

Notice that in attempting to provide an explanation of why specific arguments are good in terms of their validity, we have moved beyond simply providing quasi-natural language schematisations. Our logician has constructed a formal language whose syntax and semantics can be determined by stipulation, with the aim of modelling pertinent features of the target arguments that (putatively) allow us to explain why some are valid and others not. For instance, *Theory A*'s postulates provide a possible explanation of why Hypothesis 1 is true, and thus why instances of contraposition are valid, by (i) showing how the underlying form of these arguments ensures that whenever the premises are true, so is the conclusion, through a combination of the theory's definitions, representation rules, and Law 1, and then subsequently (ii) using these results to show how arguments of this form are *valid*, in virtue of Law 2.

Now, importantly, while *Theory A* offers one possible explanation of the truth of Hypothesis 1, it is not the *only* theory that does so. It is not difficult to build a theory that accommodates this particular generalisation and provides a potential explanation of its truth. Indeed, there are infinitely many theories that could do so. So far, all we have done is 'fit' the theory to the data. What we need, then, is to find additional evidence for *Theory A* in comparison to competitors that also 'save the data'. This is where important features of predictivism come to the forefront, for it explains how the advocate of *Theory A* can put her theory to the test against a wider range of data.

This testing is facilitated by two factors. First, that the postulates within her theory, which putatively explain why Hypothesis 1 is true, also ensure that other arguments are valid. In principle, then, the theory can be tested against whether these *predictions* about the validity of this wider set of arguments come out as correct. Second, in virtue of the logician assuming that mathematicians' judgements over the (un)acceptability of putative proofs are a reliable guide to their (in)validity, she can subsequently use mathematicians' judgements to test these predictions resulting from her theory.

Testing a theory has three stages. First, one draws out the consequences of the theory's postulates. In the case of *Theory A*, this includes consequences such as:

Consequence 1 All arguments of the form

$$\frac{\varphi \quad \varphi \to \psi}{\psi}$$

are valid.

Consequence 2 All arguments of the form

$$\frac{\varphi \to \psi \quad \varphi \to \neg\psi}{\neg\varphi}$$

are valid.

Consequence 3 *Not* all arguments of the form

$$\frac{\varphi \quad \psi \to \varphi}{\psi}$$

are valid.

Notice that these consequences are expressed within the *object-language* of the theory, not in the terms of the data against which they are tested. Thus, in order to be tested, these consequences must be *operationalised* into testable concrete predictions regarding whether mathematicians find steps within informal proofs of the pertinent form acceptable or not. This requires using the theory's representation rules, just as scientists use representation rules to test a model against some external target system. For instance, Consequence 1 would be operationalised as:

Prediction 1 Steps within informal proofs of the form

$$\frac{\varphi \quad \text{If } \varphi \text{ then } \psi}{\psi}$$

are found acceptable by mathematicians.

While Consequence 3 would be operationalised as:

Prediction 2 Steps within informal proofs of the form

$$\frac{\varphi \quad \text{If } \psi \text{ then } \varphi}{\psi}$$

are *not* found acceptable by mathematicians.

The final stage of the process is to test these predictions against further informal proofs. Here the logician is engaged in a process of (rudimentary) data collection, considering various informal proofs and looking for putative instances of the forms of arguments contained in her predictions.[37] Further, given that some of her predictions cover what mathematicians do *not* find acceptable, she must also look at cases of 'pseudo-proofs', where mathematicians judge inferential mistakes to have been made. Good examples of these are often found in introductory textbooks.

Ultimately, if the logician finds that mathematicians' judgements fit her theory's predictions, then the theory is further supported. Inversely, if the judgements consistently contradict its predictions, the theory faces problems. The more successful the predictions, the more successful the theory. However, even a relatively successful theory need not be accepted. Theory-choice is a competitive endeavour, where theories are assessed not only based upon their absolute (predictive) successes, but their success relative to competitors. Thus, when choosing a theory, our logician must ask: which brings with it the *most* (significant) successes?

Of course, our examples have been somewhat simplistic and idealised. First, *Theory A* contains a simplified picture of how elements of the theory's object language relate to the target language. No logician thinks every use of 'not' can be modelled by Boolean negation, or that every 'if ... then ...' claim can be adequately modelled by the material conditional. Here we are entering the tricky territory of how representation rules within our logical theories work, and the idealisations logics make in formulating these rules. These are important questions which would take us beyond the scope of this section.[38]

Second, *Theory A* only provides a partial picture of what constitutes validity and, thus, only a partial explanation of why certain putative proofs are good and

---

[37] One complication here is that our logician could well be mistaken about whether an inference within an informal proof is of the relevant form, and so mistake a non-confirming instance for a confirming one. Such is the reality of data interpretation.

[38] For discussion of these matters, see Peregrin & Svoboda (2017).

others not. In particular, the theory provides no account of the quantifiers or meta-inferences, such as *conditional proof* and *reductio*. However, what matters to us here is not so much reconstructing our favoured logic in all its detail. While this could be achieved, doing so would take time and move our attention away from those features of predictivism consequential for our purposes. Any subsequent improvement upon *Theory A*, and integration of these complicating factors, would come from a continuation of this initial process: testing the theory against (un)acceptable inferences, searching for cases not sanctioned by the theory, and evaluating the theory relative to competitors.[39]

Given that revisions to our favoured theory come from the recognition of supposed anomalies, it is worth noting briefly what options our logician has when faced with purported anomalies, according to predictivism. The exact answer, of course, will depend upon a theory's stage of development. If it is still at a fledgling stage, with few successes in comparison to competitors, then several anomalies may be enough to kill it off. However, if the theory has shown itself to be successful over a period of time, with few equally successful competitors, then we have several options.

First, one could simply deny the existence of an anomaly, contrary to what's being suggested. This would normally require explaining away the putative anomaly somehow. Perhaps a mistake has been made by the (usually) reliable reasoners, in virtue of the case being tricky or some confounding factors being involved, or the data has been misinterpreted as pertinent to a law when it isn't. While the former option is seen in Sinnott-Armstrong et al.'s (1986) response to McGee's (1985) cases, the latter is exemplified by Lowe's (1987) response to the same anomalies.

Second, we could alter our theory *slightly* to accommodate the anomaly. That is, not make wholesale changes, but rather alter some idealising assumptions or representation rules to protect the theory's 'fundamental' postulates while accommodating the troublesome cases, with Bledin's (2015) reply to McGee's counterexample being a case in point.

Third, we could bracket the anomalies off as outliers. While we might hope to accommodate them or explain them away in the future, as long as the troublesome cases are not pernicious and don't impact the workability of the theory, they can be tolerated as long as we're careful when applying the theory to these tricky cases. After all, it would be irrational to reject an otherwise successful theory just because of a few anomalies. This is often what happens with the liar and other nasty self-referential cases.

Finally, one has the option of revising significant portions of one's theory. What results in this case is a state of moderate anarchy. After all, in the face of

---

[39] For further examples of the process, see Martin & Hjortland (2021).

recognised anomalies, there are multiple ways in which a theory can be revised to 'save the data'. Such moderate anarchy is palatable, however, because ultimately the resulting candidate theories must all face the tribunal of relevant data via their predictions.

So far, we can see that predictivism improves upon naïve inductivism in several regards. First, it doesn't presume that logicians have direct insight into the logical form of natural-language or quasi-formal arguments. Hypotheses must be made, tested, and assessed based upon their comparative predictive success. This explains why, even when there's agreement over the acceptability of a given argument, there is still significant room for disagreement over the logic this data supports. Thus, unlike naïve inductivism, predictivism doesn't fall foul of the *transparency* problem.

Second, with the postulated representation rules contained in a logical theory, predictivism is careful to distinguish between the object-language of the theory and that of the target arguments whose validity it is attempting to explain. Further, it recognises these representation rules can be revised in the face of anomalies. This allows it to avoid the *translation* problem.

Relatedly, predictivism does not mistake the content of the *data* with that of the *theory*, thereby falling foul of the *data-phenomenon collapse* problem. While the theory is about which arguments are valid, it is tested via judgements regarding the *acceptability* of specific natural-language arguments or informal proofs. This distinction, facilitated by the operationalisation of each theory's predictions, is what allows for the data to be treated as a *reliable* yet fallible and indirect guide for the theory's target phenomenon – the validity of arguments.

Fourth, because predictivism does not conceive of logics as simply sets of valid schemata, but rather as clusters of postulates which underwrite and *produce* the resulting set of valid forms, it is able to avoid the *incompleteness* problem. We do not need to check every prediction a logic makes, nor presume that every consequence of the theory *can* be checked, any more than we do for other (scientific) theories. To deem an argument form valid, it suffices that the validity of the form is a consequence of our most successful theory's postulates.

Finally, this same feature of predictivism allows it to avoid the problem of *extensional sufficiency*. We have already spoken about how, because logics are not defined merely as sets of valid argument forms, the theory's postulates are able to explain *why* specific argument forms, and thus arguments, are valid while others are not. This point extends to theories that agree on the extension of which (forms of) argument(s) are (in)valid, while having different explanations for why. For instance, some logician may prefer an extensionally equivalent theory to *Theory*

A, which differs in virtue of altering Laws 1 and 2 to reflect a proof-theoretic account of logical consequence rather than a model-theoretic account.[40]

In terms of the problems identified with naïve inductivism, this just leaves *bad company* and *mysterious sources* unsettled. Both are addressed by the forms of *indirect* evidence that predictivism permits. So far, we have focused on the direct evidence that can be used for and against a logic, in the form of judgements regarding the (un)acceptability of specific inferences. However, predictivism also admits several forms of *indirect* evidence that can motivate revisions to an existent logical theory. As they are pertinent to the problems raised against naïve inductivism, we focus here on two: (i) *bad company*, and (ii) *clashes with other theoretical commitments*.

Cases of *bad company* occur when logicians do not have direct evidence against the validity of an argument form F but rather reject it because admitting its validity would require admitting the validity of instances of another form F' that they *do* (putatively) have direct evidence against. The relevant logician's rejection of disjunctive syllogism mentioned above being a case in point. Thus, *bad company* ensures that, in virtue of having direct evidence against the validity of argument form F', the logician has good reasons to reject (the union of) those argument forms which require us to accept the validity of F'. In such cases, the logician is required to make *some* adjustment to her theory to ensure the troublesome form F' is invalidated.

Of course, there will be numerous adjustments the logician can make to block these unsavoury consequences, just as in cases of *direct evidence* against an argument form. Thus, bad company arguments do not themselves directly lend support to a new theory. They serve only to remove certain candidates from the table – namely, those that commit the logician to the validity of F' via F. To find discriminating support for the remaining candidates, new consequences must be drawn from each, predictions tested, and their relative successes compared. Predictivism is able to recognise the existence of instances of *bad company* and incorporate them into its account of logic's epistemology because it does not require the validity of argument forms to be assessed on a case-by-case basis. Just as certain argument forms can be accepted as valid, though not directly tested, because they flow out of our most successful theory – in other words, by keeping *good company* – so some argument forms can be deemed invalid simply because they keep company with forms we *do* have direct evidence against.

---

[40] Which exact criteria logicians use to assess the explanatory power of a given logic is an open question; see Martin (2021a) and Payette & Wyatt (2019) for discussion.

In comparison, the second form of indirect evidence, *clashes with other theoretical commitments*, is akin to what Kuhn (1977: 321–3) called 'external consistency'. Such clashes occur when we combine our logic with independently well-evidenced commitments, and it's shown that the conjunction of our theory with these commitments cannot be true. Probably the most famous of these clashes arises when we combine our logic with a theory of truth, and the incompatibility between the two is brought to our attention via paradox. In the face of this putative incompatibility, we must then either revise our logic, revise the independently well-evidenced commitment, or explain away the apparent incompatibility.

For instance, assume we've found good reason so far to accept classical logic due to its predictive success. Further, assume that we also have good independent reasons to accept both the transparency of the truth predicate and the semantic closure of our natural languages. The former, perhaps, on the basis that it allows us to make blind belief ascriptions to others (Kripke 1975), and the latter because of empirical evidence from linguistics. For a period, we may be content that our three commitments – classical logic, a transparent truth predicate, and the semantic closure of natural languages – are compatible with one another. All is well. But then, a clever associate (Curry 1942) points out that the putative semantic closure of our language allows us to form problematic self-referential sentences such as,

(C) If C is true, then $0 = 1$,

which, given our further commitments to classical logic and the transparent truth predicate, allows us to infer $0 = 1$.

Given that we have excellent reasons to reject $0 = 1$ and further recognise that variations of (C) can be used to commit us to *any claim* we don't wish to be, we conclude that one of our three prior commitments must go. In the case that we think the evidence in favour of a transparent truth predicate and semantic closure is just too strong, then it is classical logic that must be revised to block these unsavoury consequences.

Note again that many such alterations to our logic will suffice. All that is strictly required to ensure *external consistency* is to make the necessary adaptations to block the unsavoury consequences. There is a whole host of options for achieving this, including paraconsistent, paracomplete, and substructural proposals. Thus, being able to 'provide a solution' to the paradox and re-establish external consistency is not enough. Ultimately, the proposed theory must be tested against competitors via the comparative success of its predictions.

By recognising that logics, like scientific theories, are assessed on the basis of their external consistency, predictivism is able to explain the role that logico-semantic paradoxes play within logical theory-choice and thereby avoid the problem of *mysterious sources* which impacted naïve inductivism.

What we have then, with predictivism, is a non-foundationalist epistemology of *logica artificialis* built upon the actual means through which logicians justify their logics, capable of avoiding the weaknesses inherent with foundationalist proposals while also avoiding the problems we recognised with more naïve non-foundationalist proposals.

5 Conclusion: *Logica Artificialis* and *Naturalis* Revisited

Predictivism is unlikely to be perfect. Just like its predecessors, faults will be found. However, it is illustrative for our purposes in this Element for three reasons. First, it demonstrates how a detailed and informative epistemology of *logica artificialis* can be constructed by looking at how logicians justify their preferred logics. What we arrive at is a more complex picture of theory-choice in logic than that proposed by traditional foundationalist accounts.

Second, it suggests that theory-choice in logic operates more like the sciences than is often presumed. This does *not* mean that logic relies upon empirical data, as Quine's evidential holism would have it. Logic can still possess its own specific and domain-relevant evidence. However, the *mechanisms* by which logics are chosen are those we are accustomed to from the sciences: *predictive success*, *explanatory power*, and compatibility with other well-evidenced commitments. This distinction between the *methodological* features of theory-choice being shared across logic and the sciences, but not their respective *sources of evidence*, is possible because predictivism is motivated not by top-down considerations, as Quine was through his naturalism, but by logical practice. Thus, engaging in the epistemology of *logica artificialis* without relying upon traditional presumptions about logic can deliver interesting and surprising results, such as the affinity between the methods of logic and the recognised sciences.

Finally, predictivism highlights the importance of distinguishing between the epistemology of *logica artificialis* and that of good reasoning. After all, it shows that in the process of justifying their theories, logicians *presuppose* the existence of certain reliable reasoners whose judgements over which inferences are (un)acceptable are used as a reliable (if fallible) guide to which arguments are (in)valid. Justifying this presupposition is the job of an epistemology of *logica naturalis*. In the Early Modern period, it was common to appeal to the benevolence of God to justify the reliability of our natural powers of reasoning. Such an explanation will obviously not satisfy most contemporary readers. For this reason, we now have more naturalistically amiable explanations of why (some) agents are sensitive to the logical facts, and so reliable reasoners. This includes Maddy's (2007) explanation of reliable *logica naturalis* in terms of our sensitivity to those structural features of the world grounding logical facts, and Warren's (2020) attempt to ground logical facts in linguistic conventions, thereby explaining the reliability of reasoners in terms of their linguistic competency. Yet, as we have stressed in this Element, these explanations of the conditions for individuals becoming reliable reasoners will not suffice to explain how we come to know the *principles* that sanction these reliable inferences; for this, we need an epistemology of *logica artificialis*. Thus, in highlighting the role that the presumption of reliable reasoning plays within the methodology of theory-choice in logic, predictivism reemphasizes the importance of distinguishing between the epistemology of *logica artificialis* and that of reliable (logical) reasoning, and how a comprehensive epistemology of logic requires both.

In this Element, we have drawn attention to our lack of an epistemology of logic as detailed and informative as what we possess for the sciences, identified three prominent causes for this situation, and highlighted what can be achieved if we avoid these pitfalls. Our hope is that a realisation of the present situation, its causes, and the potential for an epistemology of *logica artificialis* will lead to more progress in the near future.

References

Aberdein, A. & Read, S. (2009). The Philosophy of Alternative Logics. In L. Haaparanta, eds., *The Development of Modern Logic* (pp. 613–723). Oxford: Oxford University Press.

Anderson, S. R. (1971). On the Role of Deep Structure in Semantic Interpretation. *Foundations of Language*, 7: 387–96.

Anderson, A. R. & Belnap, N. D. (1975). *Entailment: The Logic of Relevance and Necessity (Vol. I)*. Princeton: Princeton University Press.

Avigad, J. 2008. Computers in Mathematical Inquiry. In P. Mancosu ed., *The Philosophy of Mathematical Practice* (pp. 302–16). Oxford: Oxford University Press.

Ayer, A. J. (1936). *Language, Truth and Logic*. New York: Dover.

Bealer, G. (1998). Intuition and the Autonomy of Philosophy. In M. DePaul & W. Ramsey, eds., *Rethinking Intuition: The Psychology of Intuition and Its Role in Philosophical Inquiry* (pp. 201–40). Lanham: Rowman & Littlefield.

Beall, Jc (2009). *Spandrels of Truth*. Oxford: Clarendon Press.

Beall, Jc & Restall, G. (2006). *Logical Pluralism*. Oxford: Clarendon Press.

Benacerraf, P. (1973). Mathematical Truth. *The Journal of Philosophy*, 70: 47–73.

Benzmüller, C., Parent, X., & van der Torre, L. (2020). Designing Normative Theories for Ethical and Legal Reasoning: LOGIKEY Framework, Methodology, and Tool Support. *Artificial Intelligence*, 287: 103348.

Bledin, J. (2015). Modus Ponens Defended. *The Journal of Philosophy*, 112: 57–83.

Bogen, J. & Woodward, J. (1988). Saving the Phenomena. *The Philosophical Review*, 97: 303–52.

Boghossian, P. A. (1996). Analyticity Reconsidered. *Noûs*, 30: 360–91.

Boghossian, P. A. (2000). Knowledge of Logic. In P. A. Boghossian & C. Peacocke, eds., *New Essays on the A Priori* (pp. 229–54). Oxford: Clarendon Press.

Boghossian, P. A. (2014). What Is Inference? *Philosophical Studies*, 169: 1–18.

Bolzano, B. (1972) [1837]. *Theory of Science: Attempt at a Detailed and in the Main Novel Exposition of Logic with Constant Attention to Earlier Authors* (R. George, ed. and trans.). Berkeley: University of California Press.

BonJour, L. (1998). *In Defense of Pure Reason*. Cambridge: Cambridge University Press.

Burgess, J. P. (1983). Common Sense and 'Relevance'. *Notre Dame Journal of Formal Logic*, 24: 41–53.

Carnap, R. (1963). *The Philosophy of Rudolf Carnap*. Cambridge: Cambridge University Press.

Chudnoff, E. (2011). What Intuitions Are Like. *Philosophy and Phenomenological Research*, 82(3): 625–54.

Cook, R. T. (2010). Let a Thousand Flowers Bloom: A Tour of Logical Pluralism. *Philosophy Compass*, 5: 492–504.

Corfield, D. (2003). *Towards a Philosophy of Real Mathematics*. Cambridge: Cambridge University Press.

Curry, H. B. (1942). The Inconsistency of Certain Formal Logics. *Journal of Symbolic Logic*, 7: 115–7.

Dalrymple, M. (2001). *Lexical Functional Grammar*. New York: Academic Press.

Dutilh Novaes, C. (2012). Towards a Practice-Based Philosophy of Logic: Formal Languages as a Case Study. *Philosophia Scientiæ*, 16: 71–102.

Eklund, M. (2020). Making Sense of Logical Pluralism. *Inquiry*, 63: 433–54.

Etchemendy, J. (1990). *The Concept of Logical Consequence*. Cambridge, MA: Harvard University Press.

Ferrer-Comalat, J. C., Corominas-Coll, D., & Linares-Mustarós, S. (2020). Fuzzy Logic in Economic Models. *Journal of Intelligent & Fuzzy Systems*, 38: 5333–42.

Field, H. (1989). *Realism, Mathematics, and Modality*. Oxford: Blackwell.

Field, H. (2008). *Saving Truth from Paradox*. Oxford: Oxford University Press.

Fine, K. (1975). Vagueness, Truth, and Logic. *Synthese*, 30: 265–300.

Frege, G. (2013) [1893]. *Basic Laws of Arithmetic* (Vol. 1) (P. Ebert & M. Rossberg, with C. Wright, trans.). Oxford: Oxford University Press.

Gaukroger, S. (1989). *Cartesian Logic: An Essay on Descartes's Conception of Inference*. Oxford: Oxford University Press.

Giardino, V. (2017). Diagrammatic Reasoning in Mathematics. In L. Magnani & T. Bertolotti, eds., *Springer Handbook of Model-Based Science* (pp. 499–522). Dordrecht: Springer.

Goel, V., Gold, B., Kapur, S., & Houle, S. (1997). The Seats of Reason? An Imaging Study of Deductive and Inductive Reasoning. *NeuroReport*, 8: 1305–10.

Hamami, Y. & Morris, R. L. (2020). Philosophy of Mathematical Practice: A Primer for Mathematics Educators. *ZDM Mathematics Education*, 52: 1113–26.

Harman, G. H. (1984). Logic and Reasoning. *Synthese*, 60: 107–27.

Hlobil, U. (2014). Against Boghossian, Wright and Broome on Inference. *Philosophical Studies*, 167: 419–29.

Hoenen, M. J. F. M. (2010). From Natural Thinking to Scientific Reasoning: Concepts of *logica naturalis* and *logica artificialis* in Late-Medieval and Early-Modern Thought. *Bulletin de Philosophie Médiévale*, 52: 81–116.

John of Salisbury (1955). *The Metalogicon of John of Salisbury* (D. McGarry, trans). Berkeley: University of California Press.

Katz, J. J. (1998). *Realistic Rationalism*. Cambridge, MA: MIT Press.

Kneale, W. (1956). The Province of Logic. In H. D. Lewis, ed., *Contemporary British Philosophy* (pp. 237–61). London: George Allen and Unwin.

Kripke, S. (1975). Outline of a Theory of Truth. *Journal of Philosophy*, 72: 690–716.

Kuhn, T. (1962). *The Structure of Scientific Revolutions*. Chicago: University of Chicago Press.

Kuhn, T. (1977). *The Essential Tension*. Chicago: University of Chicago Press.

Larvor, B. (2012). How to Think about Informal Proofs. *Synthese*, 187: 715–30.

Lavers, P. (1988). Relevance and Disjunctive Syllogism. *Notre Dame Journal of Formal Logic*, 29: 34–44.

Leibniz, G. W. (1996) [1765]. *New Essays on Human Understanding* (P. Remnant & J. Bennett, eds. and trans.). Cambridge: Cambridge University Press.

Locke, J. (1975) [1689]. *An Essay Concerning Human Understanding* (P. Nidditch, ed.). Oxford: Oxford University Press.

López-Rubio, E. & Ratti, E. (2021). Data Science and Molecular Biology: Prediction and Mechanistic Explanation. *Synthese*, 198: 3131–56.

Lowe, E. J. (1987). Not a Counterexample to Modus Ponens. *Analysis*, 47: 44–7.

Maddy, P. (2007). *Second Philosophy: A Naturalistic Method*. Oxford: Oxford University Press.

Martin, B. (2021a). Anti-exceptionalism about Logic and the Burden of Explanation. *Canadian Journal of Philosophy*, 51: 602–18.

Martin, B. (2021b). Identifying Logic Evidence. *Synthese*, 40: 9069–95.

Martin, B. (2021c). Searching for Deep Disagreement in Logic: The Case of Dialetheism. *Topoi*, 40: 1127–38.

Martin, B. (2022). The Philosophy of Logical Practice. *Metaphilosophy*, 53: 267–83.

Martin, B. (2024). Reflective Equilibrium in Logic. *Synthese*, 58. Online first: https://doi.org/10.1007/s11229-023-04480-0.

Martin, B. & Hjortland, O. T. (2021). Logical Predictivism. *Journal of Philosophical Logic*, 50: 285–318.

Martin, B. & Hjortland, O. T. (2022). Anti-Exceptionalism as Tradition Rejection. *Synthese*. Online first: 10.1007/s11229-022-03653-7

Martin, E. P. & Meyer, R. K. (1982). Solution to the *P–W* Problem. *The Journal of Symbolic Logic*, 47: 869–87.

McGee, V. (1985). A Counterexample to Modus Ponens. *Journal of Philosophy*, 82: 462–71.

McHugh, C. & Way, J. (2016). Against the Taking Condition. *Philosophical Issues*, 26: 314–331.

Mugnai, M. (2010). Logic and Mathematics in the Seventeenth Century. *History and Philosophy of Logic* 31: 297–314.

Nosonovsky, M. & Breki, A. D. (2019). Ternary Logic of Motion to Resolve Kinematic Frictional Paradoxes. *Entropy*, 21: 620.

Parker, W. S. (2010). Whose Probabilities? Predicting Climate Change with Ensembles of Models. *Philosophy of Science*, 77: 985–97.

Payette, G. & Wyatt, N. (2019). How Do Logics Explain? *Australasian Journal of Philosophy*, 96: 157–67.

Peregrin, J. & Svoboda, V. (2017). *Reflective Equilibrium and the Principles of Logical Analysis: Understanding the Laws of Logic*. London: Routledge.

Popper, K. (1959). *The Logic of Scientific Discovery*. London: Hutchinson.

Prawitz, D. (1985). Remarks on Some Approaches to the Concept of Logical Consequence. *Synthese*, 62: 153–71.

Priest, G. (2006a). *Doubt Truth to Be a Liar*. Oxford: Clarendon Press.

Priest, G. (2006b). *In Contradiction: A Study of the Transconsistent* (2nd ed.). Oxford: Clarendon Press.

Priest, G. (2016). Logical Disputes and the A Priori. *Logique et Analyse*, 59: 347–66.

Putnam, H. (1969). Is Logic Empirical? In R. Cohen and M. Wartofsky eds., *Boston Studies in the Philosophy of Science: Proceedings of the Boston Colloquium for the Philosophy of Science* (pp. 216–41). Dordrecht: Springer.

Quine, W. V. O. (1950). Methods of Logic (1st ed.). New York: Henry Holt.

Quine, W. V. O. (1951). Two Dogmas of Empiricism. *Philosophical Review*, 60: 20–43.

Quine, W. V. O. (1976). Truth by Convention. In *The Ways of Paradox and Other Essays* (pp. 77–106). Cambridge, MA: Harvard University Press. https://www.hup.harvard.edu/books/9780674948372.

Quine, W. V. O. (1986). *Philosophy of Logic* (2nd ed.). Cambridge, MA: Harvard University Press.

Quine, W. V. O. (1990). *Pursuit of Truth*. Cambridge, MA: Harvard University Press.

Russell, G. (2019). Deviance and Vice: Strength as a Theoretical Virtue in the Epistemology of Logic. *Philosophy and Phenomenological Research*, 99: 548–63.

Russell, G. (2023). How the Laws of Logic Lie. *Episteme*, 20: 833–51.

Schechter, J. (2010). The Reliability Challenge and the Epistemology of Logic. *Philosophical Perspectives*, 24: 437–64.

Shapiro, S. (2009). We Hold These Truths to Be Self-Evident: But What Do We Mean by That? *The Review of Symbolic Logic*, 2: 175–207.

Sher, G. (1991). *The Bounds of Logic*. Cambridge, MA: MIT Press.

Sinnott-Armstrong, W., Moor, J., & Fogelin, R. (1986). A Defense of Modus Ponens. *Journal of Philosophy*, 83: 296–300.

Slater, H. (1995). Paraconsistent Logics? *Journal of Philosophical Logic*, 24: 451–4.

Soler, L., Zwart, S., Lynch, M., & Israel-Jost, V. (2014). Introduction. In L. Soler, S. Zwart, M. Lynch, & V. Israel-Jost, eds., *Science after the Practice Turn in the Philosophy, History, and Social Studies of Science* (pp. 1–43). London: Routledge.

Steinberger, F. (2020). The Normative Status of Logic. In E. N. Zalta, ed., *The Stanford Encyclopedia of Philosophy*. Online: https://plato.stanford.edu/archives/win2020/entries/logic-normative/.

Tappenden, J. (2008). Mathematical Concepts: Fruitfulness and Naturalness. In P. Mancosu, ed., *The Philosophy of Mathematical Practice* (pp. 276–301). Oxford: Oxford University Press.

Tarski, A. (1944). The Semantic Conception of Truth and the Foundations of Semantics. *Philosophy and Phenomenological Research*, 4: 341–75.

Tennant, N. (1987). Natural Deduction and Sequent Calculus for Intuitionistic Relevant Logic. *The Journal of Symbolic Logic*, 52: 665–80.

Tennant, N. (2004). An Anti-realist Critique of Dialetheism. In G. Priest, Jc Beall, & B. Armour-Garb, eds., *The Law of Non-contradiction: New Philosophical Essays* (pp. 355–84). Oxford: Clarendon Press.

Tieleman, S. (2022). Model Transfer and Universal Patterns: Lessons from the Yule Process. *Synthese*, 200: 267. Online first: https://doi.org/10.1007/s11229-022-03737-4.

Warren, J. (2020). *Shadows of Syntax*. Oxford: Oxford University Press.

Weir, A. (2015). A Robust Non-transitive Logic. *Topoi*, 34: 99–107.

Weisberg, M. (2013). *Simulation and Similarity: Using Models to Understand the World*. Oxford: Oxford University Press.

Williamson, T. (1994). *Vagueness*. London: Routledge.

Williamson, T. (2007). *The Philosophy of Philosophy*. Oxford: Blackwell.

Williamson, T. (2017). Semantic Paradoxes and Abductive Methodology. In B. Armour-Garb, ed., *The Relevance of the Liar* (pp. 325–346). Oxford: Oxford University Press.

Winsberg, E. (2019). Computer Simulations in Science. In E. N. Zalta, ed., *The Stanford Encyclopedia of Philosophy*. Online: https://plato.stanford.edu/archives/win2022/entries/simulations-science/.

Woods, J. (2019). Logical Partisanhood. *Philosophical Studies*, 176: 1203–24.

Wright, C. (1985). Inventing Logical Necessity. In J. Butterfield, ed., *Language, Mind, and Logic* (pp. 187–209). Cambridge: Cambridge University Press.

Wright, C. (2004). Intuition, Entitlement and the Epistemology of Logical Laws. *Dialectica*, 58: 155–75.

Wright, C. (2021). Making Exceptions. *Philosophical Topics*, 49: 333–46.

Yalcin, S. (2012). A Counterexample to Modus Tollens. *Journal of Philosophical Logic*, 41: 1001–24.

Zardini, E. (2011). Truth without Contra(di)ction. *Review of Symbolic Logic*, 4: 498–535.

Epistemology

Stephen Hetherington
University of New South Wales, Sydney

Stephen Hetherington is Professor Emeritus of Philosophy at the University of New South Wales, Sydney. He is the author of numerous books, including *Knowledge and the Gettier Problem* (Cambridge University Press, 2016), and *What Is Epistemology?* (Polity, 2019), and is the editor of several others, including *Knowledge in Contemporary Epistemology* (with Markos Valaris: Bloomsbury, 2019), and *What the Ancients Offer to Contemporary Epistemology* (with Nicholas D. Smith: Routledge, 2020). He was the Editor-in-Chief of the Australasian Journal of Philosophy from 2013 until 2022.

About the Series

This Elements series seeks to cover all aspects of a rapidly evolving field, including emerging and evolving topics such as: fallibilism; knowing how; self-knowledge; knowledge of morality; knowledge and injustice; formal epistemology; knowledge and religion; scientific knowledge; collective epistemology; applied epistemology; virtue epistemology; wisdom. The series demonstrates the liveliness and diversity of the field, while also pointing to new areas of investigation.

Cambridge Elements

Epistemology

Elements in the Series

Philosophy, Bullshit, and Peer Review
Neil Levy

Stratified Virtue Epistemology: A Defence
J. Adam Carter

The Skeptic and the Veridicalist: On the Difference Between Knowing What There Is and Knowing What Things Are
Yuval Avnur

Transcendental Epistemology
Tony Cheng

Knowledge and God
Matthew A. Benton

Knowing What It Is Like
Yuri Cath

Disagreement
Diego E. Machuca

On Believing and Being Convinced
Paul Silva Jr

Knowledge-First Epistemology: A Defence
Mona Simion

Emotional Self-Knowledge: How Affective Skills Reveal Our Values, Goals, Cares and Concerns
Matt Stichter and Ellen Fridland

Deception and Self-Deception: A Unified Account
Vladimir Krstić

The Epistemology of Logic
Ben Martin

A full series listing is available at: www.cambridge.org/EEPI

For EU product safety concerns, contact us at Calle de José Abascal, 56–1°,
28003 Madrid, Spain or eugpsr@cambridge.org.

www.ingramcontent.com/pod-product-compliance
Lightning Source LLC
LaVergne TN
LVHW011855060526
838200LV00054B/4353